Harper Lee's
TO KILL A MOCKINGBIRD
Student Guide

David M. Wright

MEMORIA PRESS

ABOUT THE AUTHOR

David M. Wright is the director and author of the upper school literature curriculum at Memoria Press. He teaches AP Literature and English with a focus on the Great Books. He received his master's degree in English literature from DePaul University in Chicago and holds a Classical Teacher certificate from the CiRCE Institute. He is currently working on a Ph.D. in literature at the University of Louisville. He is the founder and director of the annual Climacus Conference in Louisville. His greatest blessings are his wife and seven children.

Memoria Press
www.MemoriaPress.com

Harper Lee's
TO KILL A MOCKINGBIRD

STUDENT GUIDE
David M. Wright

ISBN 978-1-61538-819-6

Second Edition © 2017 Memoria Press | 0420

All rights reserved. No part of this book may be reproduced in any form by any means without written permission from the publisher.

Contents

How to Use This Study Guide with the Text
& Literature Notebook 5
Notes & Instructions to Student 7
Taking With Us What Matters 9
Four Stages to the Central One Idea 13
How to Mark a Book 18
Introduction 21
Basic Features & Background 27

PART ONE
Pre-Grammar | Preparation 33
Grammar | Presentation & Logic | Dialectic 33
    Chapter 1 34
    Chapter 2 39
    Chapter 3 42
    Chapter 4 44
    Chapter 5 47
    Chapter 6 50
    Chapter 7 54
    Chapter 8 56
    Chapter 9 58
    Chapter 10 61
    Chapter 11 63
Rhetoric | Expression 66

PART TWO
Pre-Grammar | Preparation 69
Grammar | Presentation & Logic | Dialectic 69
    Chapter 12 70
    Chapter 13 73
    Chapter 14 75
    Chapter 15 77
    Chapter 16 80
    Chapter 17 84
    Chapter 18 88
    Chapter 19 90
    Chapter 20 92
    Chapter 21 95
    Chapter 22 98
    Chapter 23 101
    Chapter 24 105
Rhetoric | Expression 108

Contents (continued)

PART THREE
Pre-Grammar | Preparation 111
Grammar | Presentation & Logic | Dialectic 111
    Chapter 25 112
    Chapter 26 114
    Chapter 27 116
    Chapter 28 119
    Chapter 29 122
    Chapter 30 124
    Chapter 31 126
Rhetoric | Expression 129

Memorization & Recitation 132
Master Words-to-Be-Defined List 133
Rhetoric Essay Template 136

How to Use This Study Guide with the Text & Literature Notebook

A Step-By-Step Plan

INTRODUCTION AND PREPARATION

A. First read through the Notes & Instructions to Student (pp. 7-8).

B. Read the two introductory essays, "Taking With Us What Matters" and "Four Stages to the Central One Idea" (pp. 9-17).

C. Read "How to Mark a Book" (p. 18).

D. Read the Introduction in the Study Guide (pp. 21-24), marking the text in key places according to the method taught in "How to Mark a Book."

E. Complete the Comprehension Questions over the Introduction (pp. 24-25).

F. Read and study the Basic Features & Background (pp. 27-32).

BEGIN TEXT PROPER

1. Begin with the Pre-Grammar section (p. 33). This prepares the mind, at least in some small way, for the reading and study of *To Kill a Mockingbird*, and ideally, for the Central One Idea.

2. Read through the Reading Notes closely, stopping occasionally to discuss or clarify.

3. Next, try to define as many words from the Words to Be Defined section as possible in your Literature Notebook. For meanings of words that you cannot figure out from the context given, consult a dictionary (or refer to the word in the text for more context) to help you choose the correct definition from the Definitions Bank. This vocabulary work will help you better understand and comprehend the text as you read.

4. Now, read thoroughly and well the particular section of *To Kill a Mockingbird* delineated by the Study Guide (e.g., Chapter 3), marking the text in key places according to the method taught in "How to Mark a Book."

5. Return to your Literature Notebook and finish defining any remaining Words to Be Defined. If need be, refer to the word in the text for contextual help, or in a dictionary, of course.
6. Answer the Comprehension Questions in your Literature Notebook, stopping to discuss and referring to the text when necessary.
7. Complete the Literary & Rhetorical Device Exercises in your Literature Notebook.
8. Discuss and reflect upon the Socratic Discussion Questions, referring to the text often or when necessary. These are intended for verbal discussion, and they also provide a good opportunity for you to take notes in your Literature Notebook. The teacher may also assign the questions to be answered in written form in your Literature Notebook.
9. Answer the Socratic Discussion Questions. These may be verbally discussed or answered in your Literature Notebook.
10. Complete the Rhetoric | Expression—Central One Idea section. Take the time to consider and reflect upon the Central One Idea; discuss freely, making room for disagreement as well as convergence.
11. Complete the Essay Option in your Literature Notebook at your teacher's discretion.
12. Repeat steps 1-11 for each act or section.

Notes & Instructions to Student

- This Study Guide is intended to be used with *To Kill a Mockingbird* by Harper Lee, First Perennial Classics edition, 2002, published by Perennial Classics, an imprint of Harper Collins Publishers (ISBN: 978-0-06-093546-7).

- This Study Guide is best used in conjunction with a good-quality notebook, which will henceforth be called the **Literature Notebook**. You will be expected to complete most of the activities in your Literature Notebook. And of course, the Literature Notebook will be the place for all of your notes during reading and discussion, and for all of your essays.

- Though I recommend that, ideally, you complete the entire Study Guide in conjunction with reading and discussing the text—I also recommend that you **adapt the Study Guide to your particular context**. This means you should feel comfortable using the Study Guide in a way that best suits the needs of your teacher and your class—in a manner that fits your schedule, number of meetings per week, time allowed for discussion, and total time for the unit, etc. This could mean that your teacher may have you complete fewer vocabulary words and questions, etc. This is fine, and I encourage it. I have written the Study Guide comprehensively to provide a maximum number of notes, words, and questions—so that you will have plenty of work to complete, rather than wishing there were more.

- Harper Lee divided her novel into two parts: Chapters 1-11 and Chapters 12-31. In the Study Guide, I have chosen to divide her novel into three parts: 1-11, 12-24, and 25-31.

- This Study Guide is written in such a way that it can be used for grades 8-12. If you are in grades 8 or 9, additional guidance, assistance, and adaptation will probably be helpful.

- References to the text will be cited by page number, appearing like this: (p. 27).

- Pages 21-25 in the Study Guide feature an Introduction to the novel followed by a set of comprehension questions over the Introduction. Of course it is good to complete all of the questions, but at your teacher's discretion, it may also be fine to complete fewer questions. Another good option would be to complete this section orally in class discussion, in groups, or in another manner that suits your teacher's judgment.

- You will notice that many questions ask you to quote a line(s) from the text in your answer. This will help develop your ability to find evidence in the text to support your answer. It will also develop the skill of synthesizing quoted material into your written argument, which is an important skill for analytical essay writing.

- The Reading Notes section contains some helpful notes and facts along with some of the difficult words and phrases in each act. Many words and phrases deserving explanation are given treatment in the marginal notes of the text; thus, the Reading Notes will feature just *some* of the words, but not all.

- The Words to Be Defined section contains *specific* words chosen because they are both *challenging* and *useful* for you to learn and memorize.

- Some of the essay prompts tend toward a shorter essay, and some toward a longer. Both short essays (1 page or less) and long essays (2-4 pages) are useful and helpful, depending on the intent and purpose. Your teacher will convey his or her expectations regarding the length of the essay.

- In the Comprehension and Socratic Discussion Questions, I sometimes use the words "paraphrase," "summarize," or "provide a brief summary." All of these essentially mean the same thing.

- A Rhetoric Essay Template is provided in the back of the Study Guide as another pre-writing option to help you outline your essay before you undertake to write it. The template is very similar to the Rhetoric | Expression section. Your teacher may choose to have you complete the Rhetoric | Expression section or use the guide.

- Please complete the Memorization & Recitation section at the end of the Study Guide as a kind of "final achievement" that celebrates your reading of the text and completion of the Study Guide. Perhaps more importantly, this section allows you to move on from the play with a special part of *To Kill a Mockingbird* in your heart.

Taking With Us What Matters
The Transformative Power of Reading for the Central One Idea

Sometimes our study of literature resembles a kind of clinical laboratory lesson. We encircle the text in our white coats ready to dissect the story (or poem) like a dead animal. Or if this sounds too invasive or scientific, then we *analyze* the text in order to extract the "elements of literature" (the title of a recent bigpress high school English textbook)—to know the work by studying its parts. Or perhaps we analyze simply to have a meaningful artistic engagement with the text.

All of these, though, fall short of what our true purpose and intent should be when reading a Great Work. But ironically, this very purpose may be the most overlooked. This brings to mind a few similar yet related aphorisms: What we go about searching everywhere for is often right in front of us or within us; overstimulate the senses, and they sense less; keep it simple; less is more.

What we are missing in our modern study of literature is a conscious effort to uncover the soul of the work, the *essence* from which it derives its being—a fundamental, ontological reality that I have named the *Central One Idea*. Searching for and determining the Central One Idea profoundly shapes our interaction with the work and the trajectory of our study. There are seven reasons why this is so.

First, by doing so, we honor the work. Just as we notice an innate hierarchy in the natural world, in societies, organizations, and families, we insist that a kind of hierarchy exists in the work as well: there is one idea at the heart of the story; one idea burning as the sun in its solar system, with many planets (literary elements) in rotation around it. This idea gives the work its ultimate meaning and its greatest expression. In this idea, the other elements find their raison d'être.

Second, I often ask my students, "What's in a title?" to which they reply, "Everything." Then I ask, "What's in a name?" and they promptly reply, "Everything." I repeatedly ask this not only because repetition is the mother of learning, but also because I do not want them to miss what is right in front of them: The title of a work often hints at, points toward, or outright expresses the Central One Idea.

Why parents think deeply about the name they give their child reiterates this point. Names matter; they represent the potential character and nature of the child. In this spirit, I chose the name Central One Idea carefully so that its nature and purpose would be inherent. It does not roll too quickly off the tongue, but instead demands a certain level of consciousness to express. It is *central*; it is *one*; and it is an *idea*. In other words, it is central to the work and stands above other ideas, determined then to be subideas; it is singular; and it is a complete idea, that is, a proposition with a subject and a predicate, not just a subject.

Third, when we consider the essay, the academic paper, the dissertation, or any other nonfiction work, we insist that it must have a *thesis*. The thesis is everything to that particular work—so much so that, ontologically, the work derives its being from its thesis. It is no mystery why many high school and college English teachers demand that their students underline the thesis in their papers—to combat their students' shoddy understanding of what a thesis is and why it is so important.

In the nonfiction genre especially, the title almost always encapsulates the thesis. Take, for example, the academic bestseller some years ago: *Guns, Germs, and Steel: The Fates of Human Societies*. Here Jared Diamond argues that the varied developments of human societies on different continents are the result of environmental determinism—geography, population, and agriculture—and more specifically, that Eurasian technological and economic rise and dominance stemmed from their superior weapons (guns), their diseases which weakened indigenous populations (germs), and their centralized government which fostered powerful military organizations (steel). One can almost read the title, absorb the thesis, and devote 500 pages to something else, say Hugo's *Les Misérables*.

Is a novel, play, or poem really any different than a work of nonfiction? Does not fiction express a thesis just as nonfiction? I believe it does. If not explicitly, then implicitly—for it must express *something*, and that *something* is the Central One

Idea. As well, that essential idea is that which *compels* the author to put pen to paper, or the artist to put brush to canvas. The novel, poem, or painting is simply (and profoundly) the artistic medium or rendering of the idea.

So what, then, does a Central One Idea look like? In Charles Dickens' *Hard Times*, the owner of a school instructs his students in "nothing but facts" and finally realizes that his program ruins the humanity of his students. The Central One Idea: Life should be lived with imagination rather than by an overemphasis on logic and cold facts. In Herman Melville's *Billy Budd*, a young sailor is falsely accused of mutiny. The Central One Idea: Human nature is both pure and corrupt, just as physical nature is both beautiful and harsh. (Yes, these could be said in various ways; and yes, others could be argued for, but I'll get to this in point six.)

Fourth, reading for the Central One Idea moves our methodology back toward the classical and medieval, toward what C. S. Lewis called "the discarded image." In previous ages, the *idea* and *truth* had a kind of unity and primacy that is lost in modernity. I think here of Plato and his forms, Aristotle and his organized classification of reality, Dante and his fixed and ordered cosmology. The moderns prefer fragmentation, subjectivism, and deconstruction of both the idea and truth. More comfortable with truth shattered into shards, this age insists that reality is broken and disconnected, not whole and unified.

Approaching a work of literature with this broken and distant framework means students are uncomfortable asserting any one truth about a story—too afraid to insist: *This is the fundamental idea that drives this novel*. They are more satisfied pointing out elements in the work that stand out to them rather than ascribing primacy to any one; or more often, they prefer expressing *how the novel makes them feel*. As well, they might focus undue attention on a character that they like or dislike based on whether the character behaves in a way acceptable to contemporary (politically correct) standards.

Fifth, the Central One Idea might be the primary factor in the movement from novel to *Great Book*. It is difficult to find any Great Book without a prominent Central One Idea. The book becomes timeless and great for two reasons—one, it has an important Central One Idea; and two, because that idea is expressed with masterful artistry, form, and beauty.

    Sixth, determining the Central One Idea engenders logical thought and rhetorical speech. It demands close reading and analysis, supporting evidence and proof; it generates critical discussion and rhetorical writing. The nous (in patristic thought, the eye of the heart) of a work is not always easy to find. Sometimes it is everywhere present but cannot be directly seen. Sometimes it has to be wrestled for in the midst of competing ideas. Sometimes it seems too obvious and simple. But nonetheless, teaching the work in this method requires the student to stake a claim for one central idea. The student must then defend his or her Central One Idea with evidence from the text, the Study Guide, scholarly sources, or his/her own logic. And this stimulates fruitful class discussion and debate, and leads directly to the essay and composition.

    Finally, reading for the Central One Idea is the essential way to study literature because it is an act of discovery. Since we desire by nature to know, we experience joy when we discover new things and complete gaps in logical sequences. We seek so that we may find. The joy of learning comes from the Elysian fount of discovery. May we let our search for and insistence upon the Central One Idea become the *logos* of our study of the Great Works, and find there wisdom and virtue.

Four Stages to the Central One Idea
Using the Trivium to Uncover the Heart of a Work

UNDERSTANDING THE SEQUENCE AND STAGES OF THE STUDY GUIDE

Because discovering and internalizing the Central One Idea in a Great Work is vital for a proper reading and for cultivating wisdom and virtue, it necessitates that the Study Guide embody this conceptual framework. Thus, the guide is written in such a way as to lead the student (and teacher) through four stages to the acquisition and expression of the Central One Idea.

The four-stage sequence is rooted in the trivium—grammar, logic, and rhetoric—which has vestiges from the order and way of learning spanning several ages since antiquity. In the trivium, grammar is language; logic (dialectic) is thought; and rhetoric is expression. Put another way, in the grammar stage, one accumulates the fundamental elements, features, and facts of a body of knowledge. In the logic stage, one arranges, connects, organizes, compares, and reasons with the facts learned and draws a conclusion(s). In the rhetoric stage, one expresses that conclusion/truth to others.

Sister Miriam Joseph defined the trivium as the three arts of language pertaining to the mind: grammar is the art of inventing and combining symbols; logic is the art of thinking; and rhetoric is the art of communication.[1] She also states it in this way: grammar is concerned with the thing-as-it-is-symbolized; logic is concerned with the thing-as-it-is-known; and rhetoric is concerned with the thing-as-it-is-communicated.[2]

The trivium, she says, is the organon, or instrument, of all education at all levels because the arts of grammar, logic, and rhetoric govern the means of communication—namely reading, writing, speaking, and listening. She adds, "Because communication involves the simultaneous exercise of logic,

---

[1] Sister Miriam Joseph. *The Trivium: The Liberal Arts of Logic, Grammar, and Rhetoric.* Ed. by Marguerite McGlinn. (Philadelphia: Paul Dry Books, 2002) 3.
[2] Ibid., 9.

grammar, and rhetoric, these three arts are the fundamental arts of education, of teaching, and of being taught. Accordingly, they must be practiced simultaneously by the teacher and pupil."[3]

As well, the trivium is a movement from distinct parts into synthesized whole. The three stages guide the student to relate the facts learned into a unified, organic whole. This encompasses the aim and purpose of this guide—to move from elements and parts toward the unity and wholeness of the Central One Idea.

Marguerite McGlinn, introducing Joseph's work, says, "The trivium teaches us that language evolves from the very nature of being human. ... We invent symbols to express the range of practical, theoretical, and poetical experiences that make up our existence. ... Words are characterized by their relationship to being and to each other. When a speaker or writer uses a word, thus assigning it a particular meaning, it becomes a term and enters the realm of logic. ... The linguistic symbol is then translated into a logical entity ready to take its place in a proposition."[4]

We can see, then, that the trivium has much to do with being human, with negotiating our lives. It has an ontological reality within us through our use of reason and language. The four-stage sequence developed for these Study Guides is trivium-based because the trivium embodies how we think, how we learn, and how we communicate.

In our particular context of studying a Great Work, the teacher has firmly in mind the abstract singular truth that he or she wishes the student to learn, which is the Central One Idea of the work. Several other salient ideas inherent in the work will be discovered and learned along the way, but it is the Central One Idea that is the ultimate aim and purpose of the study. Knowing the destination is vitally important in this four-stage sequence. Though popular culture may be fond of saying, "It's not the destination that counts, but the journey"—nothing should be further from classical teaching and learning. Both the journey

---

[3] Ibid., 6-7.
[4] Ibid., viii.

and the destination count, but especially the destination, which is the understanding and expression of the idea.

THE FOUR STAGES PROCEED AS FOLLOWS:
Stage 1: Pre-Grammar | Preparation

To begin, the Pre-Grammar stage prepares the student for receiving and understanding the Central One Idea by invoking his prior knowledge, experience, or interests concerning that idea. Just as Socrates believed that the truth he wanted his interlocutor to understand was already within him, in some way or part, the Central One Idea is already the soil within the student. Thus, it is helpful to cultivate the soil in preparation for planting the seed. In this preparatory stage, the student is merely asked a few questions about something related to the Central One Idea, or simply about the basic plot or subject of the work—to set him thinking in a certain direction. The Study Guide features two or three questions that aim to do this, but may be supplemented with different questions or with discussion as the teacher sees fit. This is the shortest stage and can take as little as five minutes (though fine if longer).

Stage 2: Grammar | Presentation

In the Grammar stage, the student is presented with and discovers essential facts, elements, and features of the story (or play, poem, etc.). Here the student encounters many useful facts in the Reading Notes and learns new vocabulary words in the Words to Be Defined section. In addition, the student becomes grounded in the basic features of the story through the Comprehension Questions and learns new literary and rhetorical terms (that appear in bold throughout both the Grammar and Logic sections). In this stage, the student is presented with the basic grammatical units—facts, elements, features, ideas—that comprise the work. She begins to familiarize her mind with new subject matter. New *types* or *particulars* are presented and discovered here.

Stage 3: Logic | Dialectic

In the Logic stage, the student *reasons* with the facts, elements, and features of the story/poem; sorts, arranges, compares, and connects ideas—and begins to uncover and determine the Central One Idea. He *compares* the new ideas and facts with similar things already in the mind, which gives rise to new conclusions. Importantly, the final conclusion, the Central One Idea, is often an *abstract* or *general* truth, though it may be expressed by means of a story's particulars, such as a character's action and discovery, etc. The best method for leading the student toward this new abstract truth is through the Socratic method. Hence, this stage features Socratic Discussion Questions, which are different than the Comprehension Questions in the previous stage because they go further up and further in to abstract thought. Simply put, they are deeper questions with the intent of leading the student toward the Central One Idea. The Socratic Discussion Questions are intended for verbal discussion, and they also provide a good opportunity for the student to develop his note-taking skills in the Literature Notebook. The teacher may also assign the questions to be answered in written form in the Literature Notebook.

At the end of this stage, the student should be ready to make a determination of what he thinks is the Central One Idea. This is not always easy, but the student should be encouraged to take this step, a kind of "leap of faith"—though not a huge leap over a dark chasm, but a short step relying on logic and evidence from close reading, work in the Study Guide, notes in his Literature Notebook, and attentive perception and reflection.

It should be noted here that this general truth may now be exemplified in new cases and applied to new circumstances, one of which will be the expression and defense of the Central One Idea in the rhetoric stage.

Stage 4: Rhetoric | Expression

In the final stage, the student expresses what she believes to be the Central One Idea. The student's ability to organize and express her thoughts in the Literature Notebook is an important skill in the Rhetoric/Expression stage, though the essay template in the workbook works well, too.

In this section, the first question asks the student to briefly summarize the plot, and the second question asks the student to express the Central One Idea in a complete sentence. The reason for this is so the student will be forced to distinguish between a plot summary and the Central One Idea. The two are quite different. The former, of course, concerns the sequence of events in the story. The latter concerns a larger *abstract* truth—the central proposition at the heart of the story.

The third question asks the student to list three supporting points for her determination of the Central One Idea. The fourth and fifth ask for the opening lead and the closing amplification. Finally, there is space in the workbook for the student to write the teacher's version of the Central One Idea—which is helpful for several reasons, the first of which is that it enables the student to draw a comparison.

In the last section of the Rhetoric stage, the student is presented with the opportunity to write an essay—to express her Central One Idea, the thesis she must argue for and defend in her essay. This improves the student's writing skills and increases her rhetorical abilities. Options for other essays and writing activities are also presented.

How to Mark a Book

1. Underline all important passages.

2. Place a vertical line in the margin next to very important passages which you have already underlined.

3. Place an asterisk next to key passages which you have already underlined and which already have a vertical line in the margin next to them.

4. Make notes in the margin to indicate important points made in the text.

Example:

    Mortimer Adler points out in *How to Read a Book* that <u>reading is a conversation between the reader and the author.</u> You read a book, presumably, in order to learn from the author, but this process is not just a passive process on your part. The reader understands, questions, and sometimes must argue with the author. The highest respect you can pay an author is to respond—positively or negatively—to him. The markings in a book are an expression of that.   *Reading is a conversation*

    There are several devices that can be used in marking a book or article. Each has a different purpose.

    <u>First</u>, you should <u>underline important or forceful parts of the reading.</u> This will normally be done on about 15 percent of the text. However, no more than 30 or 40 percent of text, even in a very key reading, should be underlined.   *Underline*

    <u>Second</u>, you should use <u>vertical lines in the outside margin to emphasize text that you have already underlined.</u> Normally, no more than about 10 to 25 percent of the text you underlined in any reading should be marked in this way.   *Use vertical lines*

    <u>Third</u>, you should <u>mark any text that stands out as one of the one to three most important statements in the book, chapter, or article. This will be text you have already marked with a vertical line in the margin. Mark it again, using a star, asterisk, or other doodad.</u> If the passage is truly extraordinary, you can mark it with two of these markings. If it is life-changing, you might even try three, but you should find one of these very seldom.   *Use asterisks*   `*`

    <u>Fourth</u>, you should <u>make notes and write numbers in the margin. Making notes can reduce a complicated part of the text to a simple statement</u> or record a question that a passage raises in your mind. <u>Numbers can also be used to record a sequence of major points</u> or to indicate where else in the book the author makes the same points.   *Write notes (or numbers) in the margin.*

    You can also put a double line for any text that is not only important, but quotable or aptly stated.   ‖

Introduction

"Until I feared I would lose it, I never loved to read. One does not love breathing."
— Scout, *To Kill a Mockingbird*

The Life and Times of Harper Lee & the Creation of the Novel

Nelle Harper Lee was born on April 28, 1926, in Monroeville, Alabama, a small town in Monroe county between Montgomery and Mobile. She was the youngest of four children, having two sisters, Alice and Louise, and a brother, Edwin.

Harper Lee's father, Amasa Lee, was a descendant of General Robert E. Lee. He met Harper's mother, Frances Finch, while he was in Finchburg, Alabama, a town founded by the Finch family a generation before. They were married in 1912, as Amasa was beginning to prepare for a career in law. He passed the Alabama bar in 1915 and began working as a lawyer. In one of his early cases, he unsuccessfully defended two African American men, a father and son, who had been accused of murdering a white storekeeper. They were both hanged. Amasa later served on the Alabama State Legislature, and held the office of editor for the *Monroe Journal* for nearly two decades.

During her childhood years in Monroeville, Harper Lee was a tomboy and an avid reader. She enjoyed playing with her friend and neighbor Truman Capote, who would later become, along with Lee, one of America's most famous writers, in particular for his genre-creating non-fiction novel *In Cold Blood*.

After graduating high school, Lee attended Huntingdon College in Montgomery, Alabama. Following a brief time there, she transferred to the University of Alabama, where she continued to develop her interest in English literature and in writing. During the later part of her time there from 1946-1949, she began working on a law degree, and also studied briefly at Oxford University in England on an exchange program. She eventually left for New York City without her law degree to pursue her love of writing.

During the 1950s in New York, Lee worked for Eastern Airlines as a reservation clerk while also pursuing her writing. She submitted several essays and stories to publishers, but they were rejected—the usual experience for most first-time writers. In these years, she lived on very little and traveled home frequently to care for her ailing father.

In the mid-1950s, Lee became friends with Michael Martin Brown, a Broadway composer and lyricist, and his wife, Joy. In 1956 the Browns gifted Lee with an impressive Christmas present: the willingness to support her for a year so that she could devote herself to full-time writing. Lee accepted their offer and dedicated all of her time to writing. The Browns also helped her acquire an agent.

The agent took a particular interest in one of Lee's short stories and suggested she develop it into a novel. By the end of the year, she had finished a draft of the novel, which was ultimately titled *To Kill a Mockingbird*.

The publisher who reviewed the novel could see its potential, but also believed it needed to be reworked. Lee, with the help of her editor, spent the next two and a half years revising the novel. Her hard work paid off; in 1960, the novel was published. *To Kill a Mockingbird* became an immediate hit and widespread bestseller. In 1961, just a year later, the novel was awarded the Pulitzer Prize. In 1962, the novel was made into a movie starring Gregory Peck.

Lee has always been an intensely private person. Since the novel's publication, she has given very few interviews. She prefers to let the novel speak for itself. And though she attempted to write a few more works in the following years, she never finished them. *To Kill a Mockingbird* remained her only published work for about 55 years. In early 2015, news broke that a second novel by Lee would be released in July 2015. Though her new book, entitled *Go Set a Watchman*, is sometimes characterized as a sequel to *To Kill a Mockingbird*, it was actually written in the mid-1950s, before Lee wrote *To*

Kill a Mockingbird. It seems that she put the manuscript down when her editor suggested that she write another novel from the young Scout Finch's perspective, which became *To Kill a Mockingbird*. *Go Set a Watchman* was lost for several decades until it was only recently discovered by Lee's lawyer. It includes many characters from *To Kill a Mockingbird*, but tracks an adult Scout Finch twenty years after the events in *To Kill a Mockingbird*.

To Kill a Mockingbird has remained one of America's best-loved and most-respected works of literature. In a 1999 poll, librarians named it their favorite novel of the twentieth century. As well, a 1991 Library of Congress survey showed that the novel ranked second, behind the Bible, as the book that made the most difference in peoples' lives.

One of the earliest reviews of the novel appeared in *The Chicago Tribune* in 1960, entitled "Engrossing first novel of rare excellence." Here is an excerpt from the review:

> *There is wit, grace, and skill in the telling. From the narrator on, every person in the book is every moment alive in time and place. Maycomb, Ala., itself comes alive, as a town abundantly inhabited by individual human beings, each one possessed of his or her own thoroughly convincing nature and personality. And each one contributes to the quiet, sustained humor, the occasionally intense drama, the often taut suspense which all rise out of this rich and variegated complex of human relationships.*

The novel reveals some interesting autobiographical parallels with Lee's own life. As noted earlier, Lee's father, Amasa, was a lawyer who began his career with a case freighted with racial and sociological implications. In the novel, Atticus Finch is Scout's father, a lawyer who represents Tom Robinson, an African American man accused of raping a white woman. As well, Atticus's last name, Finch, is Lee's mother's maiden name. Dill, a key adolescent character in the novel, is patterned after Lee's childhood friend Truman Capote. And the setting of the novel, Maycomb, Alabama, in the 1930s, greatly resembles Lee's small town of Monroeville, Alabama.

But perhaps most importantly, there is Scout, the tomboy narrator, aged 6 to 9 while the story takes place, but who tells the story as an adult. Scout is certainly modeled after Lee as a child, and also after Lee as an adult writer. This similarity makes the novel especially autobiographical.

In *To Kill a Mockingbird*, Lee uses a captivating plot and interesting characters to explore racism and civil rights in the segregated South in the 1930s. The novel is unique in that it is both a critical examination of racism and a bildungsroman, a coming-of-age story.

COMPREHENSION QUESTIONS
(over the preceding Introduction on pp. 21–24)

1. Nelle Harper Lee was born in ___, in the year ___.
2. Harper Lee's father, ___, was a descendant of ___.
3. Harper Lee's mother's name was ___. She and Harper's father were married in ___.
4. What was one of Mr. Lee's early cases that probably made an impression on the young Harper Lee?
5. During her childhood years in her small hometown, Harper Lee was a ___ and an ___.
6. Who was Harper Lee's close childhood friend?
7. He also became a famous ___, especially for his work of literary non-fiction called ___.
8. Lee attended college at ___, the ___, and ___.
9. What were two of Lee's major interests in college?
10. She eventually left the university and moved to ___ to pursue her love of ___.
11. What fortunate opportunity presented itself to Lee in the mid-1950s?
12. Lee's agent took a special interest in one of her ___ and suggested she develop it into a novel.
13. Lee's hard work paid off. In ___ her novel, ___, was published.
14. The novel became an immediate bestseller, winning the ___ in 1961.

15. Identify one of the reasons given for why the novel remains one of America's best-loved works of literature.
16. What was the title of the 1960 review in *The Chicago Tribune*?
17. Choose one sentence from the *Chicago Tribune* review excerpt that strikes you as particularly insightful.
18. Atticus Finch is modeled after ___, and Scout's friend Dill is modeled after ___.
19. The setting of the novel, Maycomb, Alabama, in the ___ is strikingly similar to ___, the small town where Lee grew up.
20. The most obvious autobiographical parallel is that which exists between Scout, the narrator of the story, and ___.
21. The novel explores ___ and ___ in the segregated South.
22. The novel is unique in that it is both a critical examination of ___ and a ___, a coming-of-age story.

Basic Features & Background

CHARACTERS

1. **Atticus Finch** – the widowed father of Scout and Jem; the Maycomb lawyer assigned to represent Tom Robinson
2. **Calpurnia** – the African American housekeeper of the Finches; a strong, wise, motherly figure to Scout and Jem; teaches Scout how to write
3. **"Scout"** (Jean Louise Finch) – The narrator of the story. Scout is aged 6 to 9 when the events take place, though she narrates the story as an adult. Scout is a scrappy young girl, and somewhat of a tomboy.
4. **"Jem"** (Jeremy Atticus Finch) – Scout's older brother. Jem is aged 10 to 13 while the story takes place. He looks out for his sister, Scout, and they are close. As an adolescent and teenager in the story, Jem has to struggle through some difficult issues.
5. **Dill** (Charles Baker Harris) – Jem and Scout's close friend in their neighborhood. Dill spends each summer with his aunt, Miss Rachel Haverford. The rest of the year he lives in Meridian, Mississippi.
6. **Tom Robinson** – the African American man on trial for rape
7. **Arthur "Boo" Radley** – The mysterious man who lives at home with the Radleys. He rarely comes out of the house and causes all sorts of speculation and fear in the community. The Radley house is three doors to the south of the Finches.
8. **Nathan Radley** – Boo Radley's brother, who returns home from Pensacola to live with the family after Mr. Radley dies
9. **Mr. and Mrs. Radley** – the parents of Boo and Nathan Radley
10. **Miss Stephanie Crawford** – the neighborhood scold (gossip)
11. **Miss Caroline Fisher** – Scout's first grade teacher; 21 years old; new to teaching and new to Maycomb

12. **Walter Cunningham, Jr.** – Scout's classmate; the son of Mr. Cunningham
13. **Mr. Cunningham** – a poor farmer who does not take anything he cannot pay back; meets with Atticus about his entailment and pays Atticus with stovewood, hickory nuts, smilax and holly, etc.
14. **Mrs. Henry Lafayette Dubose** – a mean old woman who lives two doors up from the Finches
15. **Miss Maudie Atkinson** – lives across the street from the Finches; an avid gardener who spends quite a bit of time talking to Scout and Jem; open-minded and helps the children think wisely through difficult events
16. **Mr. Avery** – a boarder who lives across the street from Mrs. Henry Lafayette Dubose
17. **Aunt Alexandra** – Atticus's sister; comes to stay with Atticus for a few months during the trial
18. **Uncle Jack** – Atticus's brother
19. **Francis** – Aunt Alexandra's grandson; one year older than Scout in age
20. **Mr. Heck Tate** – the sheriff of Maycomb
21. **Mr. Braxton Underwood** – The owner and editor of *The Maycomb Tribune*. Though he is prejudiced, he defends Tom's right to a fair trial, and he protects Atticus outside the jail with a double-barrel shotgun.
22. **Judge John Taylor** – the judge at Tom's trial; appoints Atticus to defend Tom
23. **Reverend Sykes** – the pastor of Calpurnia's church, First Purchase African M.E. Church; takes Scout and Jem into the balcony with him at the trial, and helps them understand the trial
24. **Lula** – a rather mean parishioner at Calpurnia's church who does not welcome Scout and Jem when they attend a service there
25. **Mr. Dolphus Raymond** – a citizen who lives on the outskirts of town with African Americans; has several mixed-race children, and often pretends to be drunk to give the townspeople a "reason" for why he lives the way he does

26. **Mr. Horace Gilmer** – the prosecuting attorney who represents the Ewells
27. **Mr. Bob Ewell** – the father of the Ewell family; spends his welfare money on alcohol; claims to have seen Tom attacking Mayella
28. **Mayella Ewell** – the 19-year-old daughter of Bob Ewell; accuses Tom of attacking her
29. **Burris Ewell** – one of the Ewell children; comes to school only on the first day of each school year
30. **Mr. Link Deas** – Tom and Helen Robinson's employer; stands up for their character by shouting out from the audience in court
31. **Mrs. Grace Merriweather** – a devout Methodist and member of Aunt Alexandra's missionary circle
32. **Mrs. Gertrude Farrow** – another lady at the missionary circle; *"the second most devout lady in Maycomb"*
33. **Miss Gates** – Scout's third grade teacher
34. **Cecil Jacobs** – a schoolmate of Scout and Jem; scares them on the way to the Halloween pageant

SETTING

The Great Depression – Lee sets her story during the Great Depression of the 1930s. The Great Depression was a severe worldwide economic depression that lasted for about ten years. It was the direst, longest-lasting economic plummet in the Western world in the twentieth century.

LITERARY & RHETORICAL DEVICES

1. **action verbs** – verbs that express physical or mental action. Action verbs convey direct, succinct action, and add force and clarity to sentences.
2. **adianoeta** – a kind of irony—an expression that, in addition to the obvious meaning, carries a second, subtle meaning (often at variance with the ostensible meaning)[1]

---

[1]. "Adianoeta." *Silva Rhetoricae.* http://rhetoric.byu.edu/Figures/A/adianoeta.htm

3. **allusion** – reference to any person, place, or thing (literary, historical, or actual)
4. **antithesis** – A rhetorical device that features contrasting words or phrases in a strong parallel structure. Example from Dickens' *A Tale of Two Cities*: "It was the best of times, it was the worst of times."
5. **asyndeton** – a rhetorical device in which one or several conjunctions are omitted in order to create energy or emphasis
6. **auxesis** – A rhetorical device in which words or clauses are arranged in increasing intensity of meaning. It is a kind of *climax*, *incrementum*, or *amplification*.
7. **bildungsroman** – German for "novel of formation"; the subject of these novels is the development of the protagonist's mind and character in the passage from childhood through varied experiences, often including a spiritual crisis, into maturity.[2]
8. **central one idea** – the central, most important idea in a poem, novel, or play
9. **climax** – the moment of highest and greatest tension in the story
10. **conclusion** (also called **resolution** or **dénouement**) – "the untying of the knot"; the conclusion or resolution that follows the climax
11. **contrast** – A rhetorical device by which one element (idea or object) is thrown into opposition to another for the sake of emphasis or clearness. The effect of the device is to make both contrasted ideas clearer than either would have been if described by itself.[3]
12. **crisis** – a moment of high tension
13. **diction** – the particular words used in a work; word choice
14. **dramatic situation** – when a character or characters are involved in a conflict

---

[2]. M. H. Abrams, *A Glossary of Literary Terms*, Seventh Edition (Boston: Heinle & Heinle, 1999), 193.

[3]. William Flint Thrall and Addison Hibbard, *A Handbook to Literature*, Revised and Enlarged by C. Hugh Holman (New York: The Odyssey Press, 1960), 108.

15. **epigraph** – a brief quotation placed at the beginning of a novel or other literary work, and which usually suggests the theme or subject of the work
16. **epiphany** – a moment of insight, discovery, or revelation
17. **euphemism** – the substitution of an indirect, mild, or vague expression for a harsh or offensive expression. Example: "But why in the sam holy hill did you wait till tonight?"
18. **exposition** – the opening portion of a narrative where the author introduces the tone, setting, characters, and other important facts for understanding the story
19. **foreshadowing** – the arrangement of events and details in a way that later events are anticipated, or shadowed, beforehand
20. **hyperbole** – deliberate exaggeration used for effect
21. **idiom** - a group of words that, through usage, have a meaning that cannot be readily understood from the individual words (e.g., *raining cats and dogs; keep tabs on*)
22. **image** – A word or series of words that refers to any sensory experience. An image is a direct or literal re-creation of physical experience.[4]
23. **imagery** – the collection of images in a poem or other literary work[5]
24. **irony** – A literary device in which a discrepancy exists between the literal words and the meaning. Put another way: when words say one thing but mean another. Note: Irony differs from sarcasm in that it is usually lighter and less harsh in its wording—though often more cutting in its effect because of its indirectness.
25. **literary device** – a technique a writer uses to produce a special effect in their writing
26. **metaphor** – A direct, implicit comparison between two unlike things (does not use *like*, *as*, or *than*). A metaphor shows that something unknown can be understood because it is identical to something known.

---

[4]. X. J. Kennedy and Dana Gioia, eds., *Literature: An Introduction to Fiction, Poetry, and Drama*, 9th Ed. (New York: Pearson-Longman, 2005), G17.

[5]. Ibid., G17.

27. **motif** – an element, such as a symbol, theme, image, idea, situation, or action, etc., that occurs frequently in folklore or in literature
28. **personification** – a figure of speech that gives human qualities to animals, inanimate objects, or ideas
29. **polysyndeton** – the use of several conjunctions in close succession ("He ran *and* jumped *and* laughed for joy.")
30. **rising action** – The part of a dramatic plot which has to do with the complication of the action. It begins with the exciting force, gains in interest and power as the opposing groups come into conflict (the hero usually being in ascendancy), and proceeds to the climax or turning point.
31. **setting** – the time and place of a literary work
32. **simile** - The comparison of two unlike things with the use of *like*, *as*, or *than*. A simile shows that something unknown can be understood because it is similar to something known.
33. **rhetorical device** – a use of language that creates a literary effect, or is intended to have an effect on the audience
34. **resolution** (also called **conclusion** or **dénouement**) – "the untying of the knot"; the conclusion or resolution that follows the climax
35. **summary** – A brief condensation of gist, main idea, or story. A summary is similar to a paraphrase, but less detailed.
36. **suspense** – anxiety created by the writer to make the reader wonder what will happen next
37. **symbol / symbolism** – a word or phrase that signifies an object or event which in turn signifies something, or has a range of reference, beyond itself
38. **title** – the distinguishing name attached to any written work
39. **theme** – whatever the general idea, truth, or insight the entire story or poem reveals

❧ PART ONE ❧
Chapters 1-11

PRE-GRAMMAR | Preparation

Prepare to think about the novel and its Central One Idea by drawing upon my prior knowledge, experience, or interests.

1. Recall some of your most memorable childhood memories. Write about a few of these memories—the people, places, events, and experiences that have shaped you.

GRAMMAR | Presentation
LOGIC | Dialectic

In the Grammar section, discover essential facts, elements, and features of the novel through the Reading Notes, Words to Be Defined, and Comprehension Questions.

In the Logic section, reason with the facts, elements, and features of the novel; sort, arrange, compare, and connect ideas—and begin to uncover and determine the Central One Idea.

PART ONE • *Chapter 1*

Chapter 1

READING NOTES

1. **"Lawyers, I suppose, were children once."** (Charles Lamb) – Lee begins *To Kill a Mockingbird* with an **epigraph**, a brief quotation placed at the beginning of a novel or other literary work, and which usually suggests the theme or subject of the work. This quote hints at a couple important ideas. Harper Lee's father was a lawyer, and she studied law as well. In the novel, Scout's father, Atticus, is a lawyer whose role is central to the main events of the story. Furthermore, Scout is a child who sees the world with the eyes of a child, but who will also come to see the world with the eyes of an adult.

2. **Maycomb, Alabama** – the **setting** of the story

3. **Atticus Finch** – the widowed father of Scout and Jem; the Maycomb lawyer assigned to represent Tom Robinson

4. **Calpurnia** – the African American housekeeper of the Finches; a strong, wise, motherly figure to Scout and Jem; teaches Scout how to write

5. **"Scout"** (Jean Louise Finch) – The narrator of the story. Scout is aged 6 to 9 when the events take place, though she narrates the story as an adult. Scout is a scrappy young girl, and somewhat of a tomboy.

6. **"Jem"** (Jeremy Atticus Finch) – Scout's older brother. Jem is aged 10 to 13 while the story takes place. He looks out for his sister, Scout, and they are close. As an adolescent and teenager in the story, Jem has to struggle through some difficult issues.

7. **Dill** (Charles Baker Harris) – Jem and Scout's close friend in their neighborhood. Dill spends each summer with his aunt, Miss Rachel Haverford. The rest of the year he lives in Meridian, Mississippi.

8. **Miss Rachel Haverford** - Dill's aunt; lives next door to the Finches

PART ONE • Chapter 1

9. **Arthur "Boo" Radley** – The mysterious man who lives at home with the Radleys. He rarely comes out of the house and causes all sorts of speculation and fear in the community. The Radley house is three doors to the south of the Finches.
10. **Nathan Radley** – Boo Radley's brother, who returns home from Pensacola to live with the family after Mr. Radley dies
11. **Mr. and Mrs. Radley** – the parents of Boo and Nathan Radley
12. **Miss Stephanie Crawford** – the neighborhood scold (gossip)
13. **chattels** (p. 4) – personal possessions
14. **eaves** (p. 9) – the part of a roof that meets or overhangs the walls of a house or building
15. **veranda** (p. 9) – a porch or balcony, often partly enclosed
16. **azaleas** (p. 9) – pretty pinkish-colored flowers
17. **flivver** (p. 11) – a small, inexpensive, usually old car
18. **beadle** (p. 11) – a church official
19. **neighborhood scold** (p. 11) – a busybody who nags or criticizes everyone and knows everything
20. **exposition** – the opening portion of a narrative where the author introduces the tone, setting, characters, and other important facts for understanding the story
21. **foreshadowing** – the arrangement of events and details in a way that later events are anticipated, or shadowed, beforehand

PART ONE • Chapter 1

WORDS TO BE DEFINED

Definitions Bank	
lacking life; flat; dull	rash; lacking good judgment
a liking; preference	vague; hazy
occurring at night	walked at a slow, easy pace
powerless; lacking strength	wishing evil or harm to others

1. Simon would have regarded with **impotent** fury the disturbance between the North and the South (p. 4)
2. were **imprudent** enough to do it in the presence of three witnesses (p. 5)
3. They **ambled** across the square, shuffled in and out of the stores around it (p. 6)
4. But by the end of August our repertoire was **vapid** from countless reproductions (p. 9)
5. Inside the house lived a **malevolent** phantom. (p. 9)
6. Once the town was terrorized by a series of morbid **nocturnal** events (p. 9)
7. The Radleys, welcome anywhere in town, kept to themselves, a **predilection** unforgivable in Maycomb. (p. 10)
8. Boo's transition from the basement to back home was **nebulous** in Jem's memory. (p. 12)

 *Read Chapter 1, marking the text in key places according to the method taught in "How to Mark a Book."*

PART ONE • *Chapter 1*

COMPREHENSION QUESTIONS

1. List five details about the **setting** of Maycomb from pp. 5-6.
2. List three details about Calpurnia from the description given on p. 6. In your answer, include a quotation of the clause that features two **similes** and underline them in your quotation.
3. Whose house is two doors to the north of the Finch house? Whose house is three doors to the south?
4. List three details about Dill from the description given on pp. 7-8. For a fourth detail, provide a quotation of the clause that contains a **metaphor** and a **simile** and underline them.
5. *In spite of our warnings and explanations it drew him as the moon draws water, but drew him no nearer than the light-pole on the corner, a safe distance from the Radley gate.* (p. 9)

    Who gave the boys the idea of making Boo Radley come out?
6. Give two details about the Radley Place (as described on p. 9). For a third detail, provide a quotation of the clause that includes **personification**.
7. What activity creates **suspense** at the end of the chapter?

PART ONE • *Chapter 1*

SOCRATIC DISCUSSION QUESTIONS (LOGIC | Dialectic)

1. *Being Southerners, it was a source of shame to some members of the family that we had no recorded ancestors on either side of the Battle of Hastings. All we had was Simon Finch, a fur-trapping apothecary from Cornwall whose piety was exceeded only by his stinginess.* (p. 4)

    What do you think might be Lee's **purpose** in revealing this about the Finches? How does it provide a kind of **foreshadowing**?

2. *Yet the tradition of living on the land remained unbroken until well into the twentieth century, when my father, Atticus Finch, went to Montgomery to read law, and his younger brother went to Boston to study medicine.* (p. 4)

    Discuss "the tradition of living on the land remained unbroken." Think about this concept in general, not necessarily attached to this story. What does it mean, and why is it important? What is gained when family members break this tradition and move to the city for other kinds of work? And what is lost?

3. *Inside the house lived a malevolent phantom.* (p. 9)

    By introducing a description of Boo Radley with this **metaphor**, the narrator goes on to convey the townspeople's perception of Boo. Do their perceptions seem correct? Or do they seem closer to fearful fantasies and legends? Why?

4. *The shutters and doors of the Radley house were closed on Sundays ...* (p. 10)

    Explain the **symbolic** nature of the Radleys' closed shutters and doors.

5. *Atticus said no, it wasn't that sort of thing, that there were other ways of making people into ghosts.* (p. 12)

    Explain the presence of **foreshadowing** in this quote. Though it is very early in your reading of the novel, do you think this quote might have something to do with the **Central One Idea** of the novel? Why or why not?

Chapter 2

READING NOTES

1. **Miss Caroline Fisher** – Scout's first grade teacher; 21 years old, new to teaching, and new to Maycomb
2. **Walter Cunningham, Jr.** – Scout's classmate; the son of Mr. Cunningham
3. **Mr. Cunningham** – a poor farmer who does not take anything he cannot pay back; meets with Atticus about his entailment and pays Atticus with stovewood, hickory nuts, smilax and holly, etc.
4. **entailment** (p. 22) – Entailment means that a property cannot be sold, devised by a will, or done anything with by the owner. By law the property passes to the heir of the owner upon his death. Entailment was used to keep properties in the main line of succession. The heir of an entailed property could not sell the land or give it to an illegitimate child. Here, Mr. Cunningham has been telling Atticus and the children that his property is entailed.[1]
5. **croker-sack** (p. 23) – a gunnysack made of burlap or similar material
6. **smilax and holly** (p. 23) – branches, foliage, and berries often used as Christmas decorations

---

[1]. "Entailment." *To Kill a Mockingbird.* http://tokillamockingbirdchaptertwo.weebly.com/glossary---entailment.html

PART ONE • Chapter 2

WORDS TO BE DEFINED

Definitions Bank	
a short stay or visit	native; originating in a certain place
had discussions; talked	
indulging or delighting oneself	uneasily, fearfully
irritations; annoyances	waived the privileges of rank

1. Jem **condescended** to take me to school the first day, a job usually done by one's parents (p. 17)
2. The class murmured **apprehensively** (p. 18)
3. should she prove to harbor her share of the peculiarities **indigenous** to that region. (p. 18)
4. I never deliberately learned to read, but somehow I had been **wallowing** illicitly in the daily papers. (p. 19)
5. Miss Caroline and I had **conferred** twice already (p. 22)
6. Entailment was only a part of Mr. Cunningham's **vexations**. (p. 23)
7. My **sojourn** in the corner was a short one. (p. 24)

 Read Chapter 2, marking the text in key places according to the method taught in "How to Mark a Book."

COMPREHENSION QUESTIONS

1. What grades are Scout and Jem entering at the start of the school year?
2. List three details about Miss Caroline Fisher. For the fourth detail, provide a quotation by her that captures her personality.
3. List three details about Walter Cunningham, Jr.
4. What happens to Scout after she defends Walter?

PART ONE • *Chapter 2*

SOCRATIC DISCUSSION QUESTIONS (LOGIC | Dialectic)

1. *Until I feared I would lose it, I never loved to read. One does not love breathing.* (p. 20)

   Explain this quote.

2. *Our teacher says Miss Caroline's introducing a new way of teaching. She learned about it in college. It'll be in all the grades soon. You don't have to learn much out of books that way —* (p. 20)

   Miss Caroline's "new way of teaching" could be viewed as *modern* or *progressive* education; while Calpurnia's method of teaching Scout penmanship might be viewed as *classical* or *traditional* education. Using only the details given by Scout in this chapter, briefly describe the characteristics of these two methods. In your explanation, include a short quotation that represents each particular method. Which one worked the best for Scout?

Chapter 3

READING NOTES

1. **Burris Ewell** – one of the Ewell children; comes to school only on the first day of each school year
2. **contemptuous** (p. 30) – disrespectful; scornful
3. **contentious** (p. 30) – tending to strife; quarrelsome
4. **fractious** (p. 32) – grumpy; irritable
5. **concede** (p. 35) – to admit; to acknowledge
6. **last will and testament** (p. 35) – the final written will before a person dies
7. **diction** (p. 35) – the choice of words used in speech or writing

WORDS TO BE DEFINED

Definitions Bank	
the act of distributing	unpredictable; inconsistent
moral or social disapproval	extraordinarily small
presenting and explaining in detail	patronizingly superior behavior or attitude
sins; immoral actions	

1. Jem's free **dispensation** of my pledge irked me (p. 26)
2. Atticus was **expounding** upon farm problems (p. 27)
3. when she was furious Calpurnia's grammar became **erratic**. (p. 27)
4. staying behind to advise Atticus of Calpurnia's **iniquities** was worth a solitary sprint past the Radley Place. (p. 28)
5. The boy's **condescension** flashed to anger. (p. 30)
6. He was among the most **diminutive** of men (p. 30)
7. I'm afraid our activities would be received with considerable **disapprobation** (p. 35)

PART ONE • Chapter 3

 Read Chapter 3, marking the text in key places according to the method taught in "How to Mark a Book."

COMPREHENSION QUESTIONS

1. What **dramatic situation** takes place at the beginning of Chapter 3? How is the situation resolved?
2. Why can't Walter pass the first grade?
3. *She was furious, and when she was furious Calpurnia's grammar became erratic. When in tranquility, her grammar was as good as anybody's in Maycomb.* (p. 27)
   Why did Calpurnia request Scout's presence in the kitchen? Provide a brief quote from Calpurnia's admonition to Scout.
4. Describe the **dramatic situation** with Burris Ewell. How does it end?
5. *When I passed the Radley Place for the fourth time that day — twice at a full gallop — my gloom had deepened to match the house.* (p. 31)
   Briefly explain the **metaphor** used here. Why is the metaphor effective?

SOCRATIC DISCUSSION QUESTIONS (LOGIC | Dialectic)

1. *… but the prospect of spending nine months refraining from reading and writing made me think of running away.* (p. 31)
   What is **ironic** about what Scout says here?
2. *"First of all," he said, "if you can learn a simple trick, Scout, you'll get along a lot better with all kinds of folks."* (p. 33)
   What important moral lesson does Atticus convey to Scout here? You may answer by quoting Atticus. Do you think it **foreshadows** any coming event or **theme**?
3. *Sometimes it's better to bend the law a little in special cases.* (p. 33)
   What moral lesson is Atticus trying to teach Scout here? Do you agree with his point? Why or why not?

Chapter 4

READING NOTES

1. **Mrs. Henry Lafayette Dubose** – a mean old woman who lives two doors up from the Finches
2. **Group Dynamics** (p. 36) – the dynamics involved when people in a group interact with each other
3. **scuppernongs** (p. 39) – a species of grapes native to the South
4. **Hot Steam** (p. 41) – a superstitious belief in the South — the wandering spirit of a person who has died and is unable to get into heaven
5. **phenomena** (p. 43) – observable facts, circumstances, or occurrences
6. **suspense** – anxiety created by the writer to make the reader wonder what will happen next
7. **crisis** – a moment of high tension
8. **rising action** – The part of a dramatic plot which has to do with the complication of the action. It begins with the exciting force, gains in interest and power as the opposing groups come into conflict (the hero usually being in ascendancy), and proceeds to the climax or turning point.
9. **climax** – the moment of highest and greatest tension in the story
10. **conclusion** (also called resolution or dénouement) – "the untying of the knot"; the conclusion or resolution the follows the climax

PART ONE • Chapter 4

WORDS TO BE DEFINED

Definitions Bank

the act of avoiding; dodging	produced; brought about
favorable; propitious	sad; sorrowful
interfering; intruding	subduing; settling
loathsome; detestable	

1. The remainder of my schooldays were no more **auspicious** than the first. (p. 36)
2. For some reason, my first year of school had **wrought** a great change in our relationship (p. 38)
3. Calpurnia's tyranny, unfairness, and **meddling** in my business had faded to gentle grumblings of general disapproval. (p. 38)
4. He had discarded the **abominable** blue shorts that were buttoned to his shirts and wore real short pants with a belt (p. 40)
5. It was a **melancholy** little drama, woven from bits and scraps of gossip (p. 44)
6. Jem's **evasion** told me our game was a secret, so I kept quiet. (p. 45)
7. Through all the head-shaking, **quelling** of nausea and Jem-yelling, I had heard another sound (p. 45)

 Read Chapter 4, marking the text in key places according to the method taught in "How to Mark a Book."

PART ONE • *Chapter 4*

COMPREHENSION QUESTIONS

1. *Some tinfoil was sticking in a knot-hole just above my eye level, winking at me in the afternoon sun. I stood on tiptoe, hastily looked around once more, reached into the hole, and withdrew two pieces of chewing gum minus their outer wrappers.* (p. 37)

   Write the phrase that contains an example of **personification** in the quote above.

2. List some of the **details** of Scout's description of summer. Quote a line or two from her description in your answer.

3. Describe the children's game of playing "Boo Radley." Include a short quote from the text in your answer.

SOCRATIC DISCUSSION QUESTIONS (LOGIC | Dialectic)

1. *I could not help receiving the impression that I was being cheated out of something. Out of what I knew not, yet I did not believe that twelve years of unrelieved boredom was exactly what the state had in mind for me.* (p. 37)

   From Scout's description of her school experience at the beginning of Chapter 4, why does she have misgivings? Why does she mention Atticus and her uncle in comparison with her schooling? Describe her school experience and what she might be missing.

2. Explain the presence of **suspense** and/or **rising action** in the chapter. Does the chapter culminate in a kind of **climax**? How? Include a quotation from the text in your answer.

3. *"Grown folks don't have hidin' places."* (p. 39)

   How does this statement present a dash of **irony** and **foreshadowing**?

Chapter 5

READING NOTES

1. **Miss Maudie Atkinson** – Lives across the street from the Finches. She is an avid gardener who spends quite a bit of time talking to Scout and Jem. She is open-minded and helps the children think wisely through difficult events.
2. **arbor** (p. 47) – a garden alcove with sides and roof created by climbing plants or trees over a wooden frame
3. **incomprehensible** (p. 50) – impossible to understand or comprehend
4. **antithesis** – A rhetorical device that features contrasting words or phrases in a strong parallel structure. Example from Dickens' *A Tale of Two Cities*: "It was the best of times, it was the worst of times."

PART ONE • Chapter 5

WORDS TO BE DEFINED

Definitions Bank	
authoritative; masterful	instruction; improvement
calmly; peacefully	kindness; charitableness
curious; inquiring	understood without being stated; implied
foolish; stupid	

1. Our **tacit** treaty with Miss Maudie was that we could play on her lawn (p. 47)
2. she would appear on the porch and reign over the street in **magisterial** beauty. (p. 47)
3. Miss Maudie's **benevolence** extended to Jem and Dill (p. 48)
4. Jem said **placidly**, "We are going to give a note to Boo Radley." (p. 52)
5. he had the right to stay inside free from the attentions of **inquisitive** children (p. 54)
6. we were not to play an **asinine** game he had seen us playing or make fun of anybody on this street (p. 55)
7. putting his life's history on display for the **edification** of the neighborhood. (p. 55)

 Read Chapter 5, marking the text in key places according to the method taught in "How to Mark a Book."

COMPREHENSION QUESTIONS

1. List five details about Miss Maudie Atkinson from the description given at the beginning of Chapter 5. Quote a line or two from the text in your answer.
2. What big event do Dill and Jem plan in this chapter? In your answer, mention what they write on the note.
3. a) How does the event turn out? b) List three important points that Atticus teaches the children.
4. How does Atticus draw out the truth from Jem that they were making fun of Boo and laughing at him?

PART ONE • *Chapter 5*

SOCRATIC DISCUSSION QUESTIONS (LOGIC | Dialectic)

1. *"Atticus says God's loving folks like you love yourself—"* (p. 50)
   Summarize the quote.

2. *"You are too young to understand it,"* she said, *"but sometimes the Bible in the hand of one man is worse than a whiskey bottle in the hand of—oh, of your father."* (p. 50)

   Identify the **rhetorical device** used here, and then explain what Miss Maudie means. Provide a line or two from Miss Maudie in your answer.

3. *She loved everything that grew in God's earth, even the weeds. With one exception. If she found a blade of nut-grass in her yard it was like the Second Battle of the Marne: she swooped down upon it with a tin tub and subjected it to blasts from beneath with a poisonous substance ... one sprig of nut-grass can ruin a whole yard.* (p. 47)

   How can we see Scout's words about Miss Maudie as symbolic of some important ideas in the story?

4. *Miss Maudie's voice was enough to shut anybody up.* (p. 51)

   Why does Scout say this? What is it about Miss Maudie's voice?

5. How does Miss Maudie help Scout to see past the suspicious gossip and hearsay about Arthur Radley? Quote a line from the text in your answer.

Chapter 6

READING NOTES

1. **Mr. Avery** – a boarder who lives across the street from Mrs. Henry Lafayette Dubose
2. **ensuing** (p. 57) – following; resulting
3. **collards** (p. 58) – leafy green cabbage
4. **euphemism** – The substitution of an indirect, mild, or vague expression for a harsh or offensive expression. Example: "But why in the sam holy hill did you wait till tonight?" (p. 58)
5. **hyperbole** – deliberate exaggeration used for effect
6. **allusion** – a reference to any person, place, or thing (literary, historical, or actual)
7. **irony** – A literary device in which a discrepancy exists between the literal words and the meaning. Put another way: when words say one thing but mean another.

PART ONE • Chapter 6

WORDS TO BE DEFINED

Definitions Bank

to make a soft, indistinct sound
bleak; dismal
declining; diminishing
dilapidated; decrepit
required; compelled
spiteful; malevolent
summoning; gesturing

1. I moved faster when I saw Jem far ahead **beckoning** in the moonlight. (p. 58)
2. a **ramshackle** porch ran the width of the house (p. 58)
3. That we would be **obliged** to dodge the unseen from all directions was confirmed (p. 59)
4. the chinaberry trees were **malignant**, hovering, alive. (p. 62)
5. I lingered between sleep and wakefulness until I heard Jem **murmur**. (p. 62)
6. In the **waning** moonlight I saw Jem swing his feet to the floor. (p. 62)
7. the darkness was **desolate** with the barking of distant dogs. (p. 64)

 Read Chapter 6, marking the text in key places according to the method taught in "How to Mark a Book."

PART ONE • Chapter 6

COMPREHENSION QUESTIONS

1. List two **details** about Mr. Avery.
2. Describe some of the **sound imagery** from the children's "walk" at the beginning of Chapter 6.
3. Identify Scout's use of **hyperbole** on p. 58 and briefly quote it below.
4. *The back porch was bathed in moonlight, and the shadow, crisp as toast, moved across the porch toward Jem.* (pp. 59-60)

   What two **literary devices** or techniques are present in the quote above?

   a. antithesis; litotes (understatement)

   b. suspense; simile

   c. anaphora; hyperbole

   d. metaphor; euphemism

5. *Dill stopped and let Jem go ahead. When Jem put his foot on the bottom step, the step squeaked. He stood still, then tried his weight by degrees. The step was silent. Jem skipped two steps, put his foot on the porch, heaved himself to it, and teetered a long moment. He regained his balance and dropped to his knees. He crawled to the window, raised his head, and looked in.* (p. 59)

   Underline or write a list of the **action verbs** in the above quote.

6. What does Jem decide to do in the middle of the night? Is he successful?

PART ONE • Chapter 6

SOCRATIC DISCUSSION QUESTIONS (LOGIC | Dialectic)

1. *I lingered between sleep and wakefulness until I heard Jem murmur. "Sleep, Little Three-Eyes?"* (p. 62)

   When Jem murmurs to Scout, he makes an **allusion** to a fairy tale. To what Grimm's fairy tale does he allude? (You may need to ask an adult, look in a book of Grimm's fairy tales, or search elsewhere. After you find the fairy tale, if you have some additional time, I suggest reading it. The story is a most enjoyable read!)

2. *"Says if anybody sees a white nigger around, that's the one. Says he's got the other barrel waitin' for the next sound he hears in that patch, an' next time he won't aim high, be it dog, nigger, or — Jem Finch!"* (p. 61)

   Identify the presence of **irony** in Miss Stephanie's words above.

3. *Had Jem's pants been safely on him, we would not have slept much anyway.* (p. 62)

   This sentence begins the second section and encompasses the rest of the chapter. Identify and copy three quotes from the second section that capture the **rising action (suspense)**, **climax**, and **resolution** of the chapter.

Chapter 7

READING NOTES

1. **hoodooing** (p. 67) – practicing a kind of voodoo or magic healing
2. **whittle**(s) (p. 67) – to carve, pare, or trim (e.g., wood) into a shape

WORDS TO BE DEFINED

Definitions Bank	
deeply thoughtful; contemplative	discolored; sullied
	everlasting; never ending
hard to bear; oppressive	making sure of

1. they invented toilet paper and **perpetual** embalming (p. 67)
2. The following week the knot-hole yielded a **tarnished** medal. (p. 68)
3. and carrying it became a day's **burdensome** task (p. 69)
4. Jem no longer felt the necessity of **ascertaining** the hour every five minutes. (p. 69)
5. When we passed our tree he gave it a **meditative** pat on its cement (p. 70)

PART ONE • Chapter 7

 Read Chapter 7, marking the text in key places according to the method taught in "How to Mark a Book."

COMPREHENSION QUESTIONS

1. Why does Scout think second grade is even worse than first grade?

2. *"You've never told me anything about that night."* (p. 66)

    What important piece of information does Jem tell Scout "about that night"?

3. At the beginning of the school year, what do they find in the knot-hole? How long do they leave it there before taking it?

4. In the fall, what do they find in the knot-hole that really surprises them? For your answer, provide a quotation from the text.

SOCRATIC DISCUSSION QUESTIONS (LOGIC | Dialectic)

1. *As Atticus had once advised me to do, I tried to climb into Jem's skin and walk around in it.* (p. 65)

    What evidence from the beginning of this chapter suggests that Scout is advancing in understanding—in other words, becoming wiser? Explain.

2. *"And something else—" Jem's voice was flat. "Show you when we get home. They'd been sewed up. Not like a lady sewed 'em, like somethin' I'd try to do. It's almost like—"*
    "—somebody knew you were comin' back for 'em."
    Jem shuddered. "Like somebody was readin' my mind ... like somebody could tell what I was gonna do. Can't anybody tell what I'm gonna do lest they know me, can they, Scout?" (p. 66)

    What might this suggest about greater forces at work in the children's experience and situation? Does this **foreshadow** anything?

3. Do you think the two small images carved in soap will function as a **symbol** in the story? Why or why not?

4. How does Mr. Radley plugging the hole with cement create a **crisis** in the story? Explain. How does this action affect Jem, and why?

PART ONE • Chapter 8

Chapter 8

READING NOTES

1. **touchous** (p. 73) – a variant of "touchy"
2. **Appomattox** (p. 74) – A small town in Virginia where Gen. Robert E. Lee and his Confederate States Army surrendered to General Ulysses S. Grant and his Union Army on April 9, 1865, ending the Civil War.
3. **libel** (p. 76) – a slandering and defaming of one's character or reputation

WORDS TO BE DEFINED

Definitions Bank	
bewilderment; confusion	hurrying; hastening
confronted; addressed boldly	noisy disturbance; uproar
friendly; warm	ordered; commanded

1. Atticus finally called us to order and **bade** us look at our plates instead of out the windows (p. 73)
2. When we were on the sidewalk in front of Miss Maudie's, Mr. Avery **accosted** us. (p. 74)
3. Soft taffeta-like sounds and muffled **scurrying** sounds filled me with helpless dread. (p. 78)
4. she still took a lively and **cordial** interest in Jem's and my affairs. (p. 83)
5. She must have seen my **perplexity** (p. 83)
6. Only thing I worried about last night was all the danger and **commotion** it caused. (p. 83)

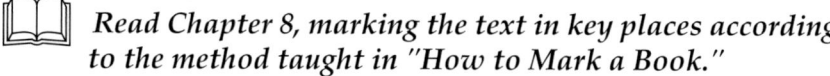 Read Chapter 8, marking the text in key places according to the method taught in "How to Mark a Book."

PART ONE • Chapter 8

COMPREHENSION QUESTIONS

1. What do the kids see for the first time that brings great excitement? What do they make out of it?
2. Why does Atticus say, *"You've perpetrated a near libel here in the front yard. We've got to disguise this fellow"*? (p. 76)
3. What big, shocking event happens in this chapter? Include a quotation from this event in your answer.
4. How does Miss Maudie react over the loss of her house to fire? What is her attitude? Include a quotation in your answer.

SOCRATIC DISCUSSION QUESTIONS (LOGIC | Dialectic)

1. *Just as the birds know where to go when it rains, I knew when there was trouble in our street.* (p. 78)

    Lee introduces important bird **symbolism** in this chapter, which runs through much of the book. What do you think "Just as the birds know where to go when it rains" might symbolize?

2. What other bird **symbols** have you come across in the novel?

3. *"… Mr. Nathan put cement in that tree, Atticus, an' he did it to stop us findin' things — he's crazy, I reckon, like they say, but Atticus, I swear to God he ain't ever harmed us, he ain't ever hurt us, he coulda cut my throat from ear to ear that night but he tried to mend my pants instead … he ain't ever hurt us, Atticus — "* (p. 81)

    What important point does Jem reveal here? How does it reveal that he is breaking down some stereotypes and beginning to see things with a more open mind?

4. How do the fire and the snow function as **symbols**? What might they represent?

5. What important object serves as yet another **symbol** for the kindness of Boo Radley? What important point is made through the use of this **symbol**?

Chapter 9

READING NOTES

1. **Aunt Alexandra** – Atticus's sister
2. **Uncle Jack** – Atticus's brother
3. **Francis** – Aunt Alexandra's grandson; one year older than Scout in age
4. **get your goat** (p. 87) – an idiom that means to annoy or make you angry
5. **Missouri Compromise** (p. 87) – The U.S. Congress in 1820 settled a debate over slavery in the Louisiana Purchase area. The compromise temporarily helped balance the slave states and the free states.
6. **Ol' Blue Light** (p. 87) – a nickname for the Confederate general Stonewall Jackson
7. **trousseau** (p. 92) – the clothes, linen, etc., collected by a bride for her marriage
8. **deportment** (p. 92) – behavior and manners
9. **obstreperous** (p. 97) – unruly, noisy, and unmanageable

WORDS TO BE DEFINED

Definitions Bank	
abusive, foul language	comparable; similar
an action or speech that makes someone angry	excessively; immoderately
	honesty; sincerity
childlike; innocent	inborn; natural

1. He wore a General Hood type beard of which he was **inordinately** vain. (p. 87)
2. he enjoyed everything I disapproved of, and disliked my **ingenuous** diversions. (p. 88)
3. Aunt Alexandra would have been **analogous** to Mount Everest (p. 89)
4. aside from the **innate** attractiveness of such words (p. 90)
5. not unless there's extreme **provocation** connected with 'em. (p. 90)
6. The internal arrangements of the Finch house were indicative of Simon's **guilelessness** (p. 91)
7. Her use of bathroom **invective** leaves nothing to the imagination. (p. 99)

 Read Chapter 9, marking the text in key places according to the method taught in "How to Mark a Book."

COMPREHENSION QUESTIONS

1. What was Scout's campaign to avoid going to school?
2. How does Uncle Jack keep Scout calm when she has to have a splinter removed from her foot?
3. What is the one thing that Scout likes about Aunt Alexandra?
4. Why does Scout think Uncle Jack is "a prince of a fellow"?

PART ONE • *Chapter 9*

SOCRATIC DISCUSSION QUESTIONS (LOGIC | Dialectic)

1. Uncle Jack learns quite a bit about Scout, Atticus, and himself. What does he learn?

2. Uncle Jack punishes Scout without first hearing her side of the story. How does this **foreshadow** the upcoming trial of Tom Robinson? By having Scout relay her experience and feelings in this situation, does it help prepare readers to understand how Tom will feel?

3. Provide a quotation by Atticus that stands out to you from his conversation with Uncle Jack in the last few pages of the chapter. Then provide a brief reflection on the quotation, stating what truth it conveys and why it is important.

Chapter 10

READING NOTES

1. **mausoleum** (p. 103) – a tomb; a building for housing tombs
2. **Jew's Harp** (p. 104) – a small mouth harp (musical instrument) that produces a soft twanging sound
3. **moseyin'** (p. 106) – sauntering; moving in a leisurely way
4. **mad dog** (p. 107) – a dog who has rabies, causing the dog to be mad and angry
5. **alist** (p. 109) – tilted to one side

WORDS TO BE DEFINED

Definitions Bank	
clear and effective in speech	unnoticeable; unassuming
with intense emotion; passionately	unpredictably; lacking regularity
leafy plants and trees	

1. With these attributes, however, he would not remain as **inconspicuous** as we wished him to (p. 103)
2. He walked **erratically**, as if his right legs were shorter than his left legs. (p. 106)
3. he was not playing or sniffing at **foliage** (p. 108)
4. Atticus shook his head **vehemently**. (p. 109)
5. Jem became vaguely **articulate**. (p. 111)

 Read Chapter 10, marking the text in key places according to the method taught in "How to Mark a Book."

PART ONE • Chapter 10

COMPREHENSION QUESTIONS

1. Using Scout's description, identify three characteristics about Atticus that make him different from other schoolmates' fathers.

2. *"I'd rather you shot at tin cans in the back yard, but I know you'll go after birds. Shoot all the bluejays you want, if you can hit 'em, but remember it's a sin to kill a mockingbird."* (p. 103)

    Scout asks Miss Maudie about Atticus's comment. According to Miss Maudie, why does Atticus think it is a sin to kill a mockingbird? For your answer, provide a direct quotation.

3. Why do the Methodists challenge the Baptists to a game of touch football?

4. How does Jem describe Tim Johnson's behavior to Calpurnia? Include a quotation in your answer.

5. How long has it been since Atticus shot a gun?

SOCRATIC DISCUSSION QUESTIONS (LOGIC | Dialectic)

1. This chapter reveals the origin of the title. a) From the explanation given, why do you think this serves as a fitting title for the novel? b) How or why does the mockingbird function as the primary **symbol** in the novel?

2. *"If your father's anything, he's civilized in his heart."* (p. 112)
    Why does Miss Maudie say that Atticus is civilized in his heart? What reasons does she provide? Include a quotation in your answer.

3. *"People in their right minds never take pride in their talents."* (p. 112)
    Do you agree with Miss Maudie? Why or why not?

Chapter 11

READING NOTES

1. **Tom Robinson** – the African American man accused of rape
2. **CSA pistol** – A Confederate States of America pistol given to veterans of the Civil War. Mrs. Dubose probably had a husband or relative who was killed in the Civil War.
3. **he went livid** (p. 115) – he became angry
4. **camisole** (p. 117) – a woman's sleeveless undergarment or shirt with narrow straps
5. **philippic** (p. 117) – a harsh verbal attack
6. **rectitude** (p. 118) – correct, upright behavior
7. **interdict** (p. 118) – an authoritative prohibition
8. **camellia** (p. 118) – an ornamental shrub with glossy leaves and white, pink, red, or variegated rose-like flowers
9. **palliation** (p. 118) – a lessening or easing of pain
10. **morphine** (p. 127) – a painkiller used to block severe pain; can become highly addictive

PART ONE • Chapter 11

WORDS TO BE DEFINED

Definitions Bank	
a long, angry speech	peaceful; calm
deterioration; decline	provoked anger in someone
extremely angry; furious	survey; examination
offense; resentment	

1. Once she heard Jem refer to our father as "Atticus" and her reaction was **apoplectic**. (p. 115)
2. we were followed up the sidewalk by a philippic on our family's moral **degeneration** (p. 117)
3. I wasn't sure what Jem resented most, but I took **umbrage** at Mrs. Dubose's assessment (p. 117)
4. he had a naturally **tranquil** disposition and a slow fuse. (p. 118)
5. He set me on my feet, and I made a secret **reconnaissance** of Jem. (p. 120)
6. I was expecting a **tirade**, but all she said was, "You may commence reading, Jeremy." (p. 122)
7. Today she had **antagonized** Jem for nearly two hours (p. 125)

 Read Chapter 11, marking the text in key places according to the method taught in "How to Mark a Book."

COMPREHENSION QUESTIONS

1. When Jem becomes furious at something Mrs. Dubose says when they walk by, how does Atticus say they should respond? Provide a quotation from Atticus for your answer.
2. What generous gift does Jem buy for Scout with his birthday money? What does he do with it that creates a major **crisis** in the chapter?
3. *Two geological ages later, we heard the soles of Atticus's shoes scrape the front steps.* (p. 119)

   Explain Scout's use of **hyperbole** here. Why does she feel it takes so long for Atticus to get home?
4. As a consequence for Jem's actions, what does Mrs. Dubose ask him to do?

PART ONE • *Chapter 11*

SOCRATIC DISCUSSION QUESTIONS (LOGIC | Dialectic)

1. *Jem was scarlet. I pulled at his sleeve, and we were followed up the sidewalk by a philippic on our family's moral degeneration ...* (p. 117)
   How does the use of **physical description** convey how Jem feels?

2. *His voice was like the winter wind.* (p. 119)
   How does the use of **simile** convey the feelings and attitude of Atticus?

3. *"Scout," said Atticus, "when summer comes you'll have to keep your head about far worse things ... it's not fair for you and Jem, I know that, but sometimes we have to make the best of things, and the way we conduct ourselves when the chips are down — well, all I can say is, when you and Jem are grown, maybe you'll look back on this with some compassion and some feeling that I didn't let you down. This case, Tom Robinson's case, is something that goes to the essence of man's conscience — Scout, I couldn't go to church and worship God if I didn't try to help that man."* (p. 120)
   Identify the most important points in this quote. What truths do they convey? Why are they important?

4. Why does Atticus want Jem to agree to read to Mrs. Dubose? Do you agree with his decision?

5. Can we see the white, waxy Snow-on-the-Mountain camellia that Mrs. Dubose gave Jem as an important **symbol** in this chapter, or even in the novel as a whole? Explain. Include a quotation in your answer.

PART ONE • Chapters 1-11

Rhetoric | Expression

Express in your own words the Central One Idea with supporting points.

RHETORICAL EXPRESSION:
To be answered in your Literature Notebook in preparation for your essay.

1. In a paragraph or two, **summarize** the major events of Part One (Chapters 1-11).
2. Write the **Central One Idea** of Part One in a precise, eloquent sentence.
3. List three or four points that **support** your determination of the Central One Idea.
4. Write a **lead** (1-2 sentences) that grabs the reader's attention—such as a *quote, question, startling fact or statistic, scenario, piece of dialogue,* etc.
5. Write an **amplification/importance** (1-2 sentences) that explains why your thesis is important in a larger or more universal sense.

◆ **Central Quote:** *Choose a quote from anywhere in Part One that you think best embodies the Central One Idea and copy it down.*

❶ **Write the Central One Idea as expressed by the teacher.**

PART ONE • Chapters 1-11

ESSAY OPTION

Choose a topic below and respond with a 3-5 paragraph essay that includes an Introduction with a clear thesis; a Body with organized, logical, and specific support of the thesis; and a Conclusion with an amplification of the thesis/support.

The essay should feature appropriate tone, voice, and point of view; correct grammar, usage, and mechanics; a variety of sentence structures enhanced by subordination and parallelism; a balance of general and specific detail; and enhanced rhetorical effect through transition words, appropriate diction, strong verbs, descriptive adjectives, and other rhetorical devices.

Note: Some of these prompts tend toward a shorter essay, and some toward a longer. Check with your teacher to see what length he or she suggests. Both short essays (1 page) and long essays (2-4 pages) are useful and helpful, depending on the intent and purpose.

1. Write an essay about Atticus and his various qualities. Take a position about Atticus as a father, leader, or person (or all three), and support your thesis with evidence from the text.

2. Write an essay about Mrs. Henry Lafayette Dubose and her various qualities. Take a clear position on her character, defending it with evidence from the text, as well as your own logical conclusions and perceptions.

3. Write an essay about the significance of the items that Boo leaves for the children. What do they reveal about Boo? What larger message comes through these actions?

4. At this point in the novel, Scout is not fully enlightened by any means. But she is gradually growing in awareness and wisdom. Write an essay about Scout's gradual enlightenment. What is she learning? How is she learning it?

5. [Central One Idea] Use the Central One Idea of Part One as your thesis, and support it with some evidence from your reading of Part One and/or your work in the Literature Notebook.

6. [Open] Write an essay in which you analyze an aspect of Part One that is of import to you, such as a particular theme, character, setting, element of plot, dialogue, symbol, or other literary or rhetorical motif.

7. [Teacher] Essay prompt.

PART TWO
Chapters 12-24

PRE-GRAMMAR | Preparation

Prepare to think about the novel and its Central One Idea by drawing upon my prior knowledge, experience, or interests.

1. Define stereotype.
2. Define racism.
3. Why are broad assumptions about groups of people not beneficial or helpful in our personal interactions with others?
4. How would you feel if you were put on trial—leading to imprisonment or death—for your skin color, your age, or your hair color? Describe some of your thoughts and feelings.

GRAMMAR | Presentation
LOGIC | Dialectic

In the Grammar section, discover essential facts, elements, and features of the novel through the Reading Notes, Words to Be Defined, and Comprehension Questions.

In the Logic section, reason with the facts, elements, and features of the novel; sort, arrange, compare, and connect ideas—and begin to uncover and determine the Central One Idea.

Chapter 12

READING NOTES

1. **First Purchase African M.E. Church** – the African American church in Maycomb; Calpurnia's church
2. **Reverend Sykes** – the pastor of First Purchase African M.E. Church
3. **Lula** – a mean parishioner at First Purchase Church who does not welcome Scout and Jem when they attend a service there
4. **habiliments** (p. 134) – clothing
5. **petticoat** (p. 134) – an undergarment worn under a skirt or dress
6. **asafoetida** (p. 135) – a gum resin from Asiatic plants, used to treat illnesses.
7. **Hunt's *The Light of the World*** (p. 136) – A well-known, allegorical painting of Jesus (1851-1854) by William Holman Hunt. It features Jesus, holding a lantern, preparing to knock on a door that looks as if it is rarely opened.
8. **ecclesiastical impedimenta** (p. 136) – church supplies and equipment
9. **voile** (p. 140) – a thin fabric of cotton, wool, or silk
10. **primer** (p. 142) – pronounced with a short **i** sound; an elementary book for teaching reading
11. **Blackstone's *Commentaries*** (p. 142) – one of the most important books ever written on British law

PART TWO • Chapter 12

WORDS TO BE DEFINED

> **Definitions Bank**
>
> condemnation; criticism severe; strict
> flighty; silly usual; traditional
> indicated; designated

1. he was diligently writing on a slate while some **frivolous**-looking girls yelled (p. 133)
2. Lightning rods guarding some graves **denoted** dead who rested uneasily (p. 135)
3. His sermon was a forthright **denunciation** of sin (p. 138)
4. an **austere** declaration of the motto on the wall behind him (p. 138)
5. It was **customary** for field Negroes with tiny children to deposit them (p. 140)

 Read Chapter 12, marking the text in key places according to the method taught in "How to Mark a Book."

COMPREHENSION QUESTIONS

1. What changes does Scout observe in Jem's behavior, and how does she deal with it? Who helps her deal with this, and how? Include a quotation in your answer.
2. Who is not coming to visit this summer? How does it make Scout feel? Include a quotation in your answer.
3. List three **details** about First Purchase Church.
4. List at least two important aspects about the service at First Purchase (that are different from what the children are used to).
5. Why does Rev. Sykes continue to ask for money?
6. Who accused Tom Robinson of raping his daughter?

PART TWO • Chapter 12

SOCRATIC DISCUSSION QUESTIONS (LOGIC | Dialectic)

1. *... but the roses on her hat trembled indignantly.* (p. 135)
   Who opposes the children at First Purchase Church? What clever one-sentence response does Calpurnia give to her opposition? Provide a quotation of her response.

2. *Behind the rough oak pulpit a faded pink silk banner proclaimed God Is Love, the church's only decoration except a rotogravure print of Hunt's* The Light of the World. (p. 136)
   Is it significant or suggestive that Lee chose to adorn the church with only two decorations, and these particular two? What might she be subtly suggesting through these?

3. Do you agree or disagree with Rev. Sykes' direct methods in dealing with his congregation? Why or why not?

Chapter 13

READING NOTES

1. **amanuensis** (p. 146) – one employed to copy down dictations or make copies of something already written
2. **caste system** (p. 149) – a class structure that is determined by birth
3. **dicta** (p. 149) – plural for *dictum*, an authoritative statement that expresses a general truth; a well-known remark

WORDS TO BE DEFINED

Definitions Bank	
difficult to catch or achieve	indirectly; in a roundabout way
dreadful; intimidating	sensitive; considerate
exclusive; privilege	shortsighted

1. I realized that this was not a **tactful** question. (p. 145)
2. From any angle, it was **formidable**. (p. 145)
3. she would exercise her royal **prerogative**: she would arrange, advise, caution, and warn. (p. 147)
4. Aunt Alexandra was of the opinion, **obliquely** expressed, that the longer a family had been squatting on one patch of land the finer it was. (p. 147)
5. Sinkfield reduced his guests to **myopic** drunkenness one evening (p. 148)
6. Atticus paused, watching me locate an **elusive** redbug on my leg. (p. 151)

 Read Chapter 13, marking the text in key places according to the method taught in "How to Mark a Book."

PART TWO • Chapter 13

COMPREHENSION QUESTIONS

1. From the information given in this chapter, list four fundamental details about Aunt Alexandra. Include a quotation in your answer.
2. In the beginning of the chapter, what does Aunt Alexandra say is the main reason for coming to stay?
3. What is the primary reason for Maycomb's existence? Why is it located where it is?
4. Why did the town remain the same size for a hundred years?
5. Reconstruction rule and economic ruin forced the town to grow. But *how* did it grow?
6. What is Aunt Alexandra's primary agenda when she comes to live with Scout and Jem?

SOCRATIC DISCUSSION QUESTIONS (LOGIC | Dialectic)

1. *Aunt Alexandra fitted into the world of Maycomb like a hand into a glove, but never into the world of Jem and me.* (p. 149)

   This illustrates an important contrast between the world of Maycomb and the world of Jem and Scout. Why does Aunt Alexandra fit so well into the world of Maycomb, but not into the world of Jem and Scout?

2. *For no reason I felt myself beginning to cry, but I could not stop. This was not my father. My father never thought these thoughts.* (p. 151)

   How does Atticus feel about Aunt Alexandra's instruction about the family history? Does he subscribe to her perspective? Include a quote in your answer.

Chapter 14

READING NOTES

1. **Hoover cart** (p. 153) – The Hoover cart was driven by North Carolina farmers as a form of transportation during the Depression and was built by taking the rear wheels off of a car and attaching them to a cart. The cart was then pulled by either mule or horse.
2. **rankling** (p. 156) – causing irritation or resentment

WORDS TO BE DEFINED

Definitions Bank	
hesitant; uncertain	strong; able to recover quickly
self-respect; pride	to call on; to appeal to
strength of mind; endurance	unerring; unfailing

1. the only way I could retire with a shred of **dignity** was to go to the bathroom (p. 154)
2. As I passed the bed I stepped on something warm, **resilient**, and rather smooth. (p. 157)
3. Jem made a **tentative** swipe under the bed. (p. 158)
4. until his **infallible** sense of direction told him he was in Abbot County (p. 159)
5. he had not the nerve to **invoke** the rule on small children traveling a distance alone (p. 160)
6. He bore with **fortitude** her Wait Till I Get You Home (p. 160)

 Read Chapter 14, marking the text in key places according to the method taught in "How to Mark a Book."

PART TWO • Chapter 14

COMPREHENSION QUESTIONS

1. Though Scout and Jem no longer hear much about the Finch family from Aunt Alexandra, they hear quite a lot from whom? Why?
2. What does Scout want to do next Sunday that is met with resistance by Aunt Alexandra?
3. **Summarize** Atticus's response to Aunt Alexandra regarding her suggestion that they get rid of Calpurnia. Include a brief quotation in your answer.
4. What does Scout step on in the dark of her room?

SOCRATIC DISCUSSION QUESTIONS (LOGIC | Dialectic)

1. *I felt the starched walls of a pink cotton penitentiary closing in on me …* (p. 155)

   How does the use of **figurative language** contribute to the way Scout feels here?

2. *Punk, punk, punk, her needle broke the taut circle. She stopped, and pulled the cloth tighter: punk-punk-punk. She was furious.* (p. 156)

   How does the use of **onomatopoeia** and the activity of embroidering convey the way Aunt Alexandra feels here?

3. *Dill was off again. Beautiful things floated around in his dreamy head. He could read two books to my one, but he preferred the magic of his own inventions. He could add and subtract faster than lightning, but he preferred his own twilight world, a world where babies slept, waiting to be gathered like morning lilies. He was slowly talking himself to sleep and taking me with him, but in the quietness of his foggy island there rose the faded image of a gray house with sad brown doors.* (p. 163)

   This is one of the most beautiful passages in the book. What words, phrases, or clauses stand out to you? What does it reveal about Dill's personality?

Chapter 15

READING NOTES

1. **Mr. Heck Tate** – the sheriff of Maycomb
2. **Mr. Braxton Underwood** – The owner and editor of *The Maycomb Tribune*. Though he is prejudiced, he defends Tom's right to a fair trial, and he protects Atticus outside the jail with a double-barreled shotgun.
3. **shinnied** (p. 165) – a slang term in the South for "liquored"
4. **pronouncement** (p. 167) – an authoritative statement; proclamation
5. **Ku Klux Klan** (p. 167) – A secret society initiated in the South after the Civil War to advocate white supremacy, often through violent means.
6. **peculiarities** (p. 169) – odd or unusual habits or features
7. **Victorian privy** (p. 171) – an outdoor toilet from the Victorian era (19th century)
8. **Jitney Jungle** (p. 171) – a chain of supermarkets that began in Jackson, Mississippi, in 1919
9. **discreet** (p. 171) – cautious; inconspicuous
10. **acquiescence** (p. 173) – acceptance; assent
11. **aggregation** (p. 174) – a group of individuals or things
12. **uncouth** (p. 174) – uncivilized; uncultured; lacking refinement or grace
13. **ramshackle** (p. 175) – dilapidated; in disrepair

PART TWO • Chapter 15

WORDS TO BE DEFINED

Definitions Bank	
concise; brief	to suppress; to smother
distinguished; grand	to take exception to; to object to
hindered; constrained	
malady; distress	unable to be heard

1. I don't think anybody in Maycomb'll **begrudge** me a client, with times this hard. (p. 165)
2. Atticus said something **inaudible**. (p. 165)
3. Atticus tried to **stifle** a smile but didn't make it. (p. 167)
4. an **affliction** Calpurnia said all boys caught at his age. (p. 169)
5. The Maycomb jail was the most **venerable** and hideous of the county's buildings. (p. 170)
6. "Called 'em off on a snipe hunt," was the **succinct** answer. (p. 172)
7. Dill was **encumbered** by the chair, and his pace was slower. (p. 176)

 Read Chapter 15, marking the text in key places according to the method taught in "How to Mark a Book."

COMPREHENSION QUESTIONS

1. Grown men stand in a front yard in Maycomb for what two reasons?
2. Who were some of the people standing with Atticus in the front yard?
3. What major event causes the men to have discussions outside on Saturday and Sunday?
4. What are Atticus's two peculiarities?
5. Describe four details about the Maycomb jail.

PART TWO • Chapter 15

SOCRATIC DISCUSSION QUESTIONS (LOGIC | Dialectic)

1. *"… in favor of Southern womanhood as much as anybody, but not for preserving polite fiction at the expense of human life."* (p. 167)

   Copy the use of **antithesis** in the quote above. Then paraphrase what Atticus says.

2. Why do you think Atticus likes to be by himself in church?

3. *Atticus had said it was the polite thing to talk to people about what they were interested in, not about what you were interested in.* (p. 174)

   How does this further reveal Atticus's character?

4. Who were the most courageous three characters in the **dramatic situation** in front of the jail? Why?

Chapter 16

READING NOTES

1. **Judge John Taylor** – the judge at Tom's trial; he appoints Atticus to defend Tom
2. **Mr. Dolphus Raymond** – A citizen who lives on the outskirts of town with African Americans. He has several mixed-race children, and often pretends to be drunk to give the townspeople a "reason" for why he lives the way he does.
3. **fey** (p. 178) – strange; unusual
4. **christened** (p. 178) – named and dedicated ceremonially
5. **Braxton Bragg** (p. 178) – commander of the Western Confederate Army in the Civil War
6. **starchiness** (p. 178) – stiffness; formality
7. **straight Prohibition ticket** (p. 181) – Prohibition was a period in U.S. history from 1920-1933 when it was illegal to manufacture, transport, import, or sell alcoholic beverages in any form. In this context, Mr. Tensaw Jones voted for political candidates who support Prohibition.
8. **akimbo** (p. 181) – a manner of standing with hands on hips and elbows extending outward
9. **William Jennings Bryan** (p. 182) – (1860-1925) a politician, lawyer, and orator whose speeches were major events in the South
10. **subpoena** (p. 182) – a legal writ or tool requiring a person to appear in court
11. **gala** (p. 182) – a festive celebration
12. **champertous connivance** (p. 188) – Derives from "champerty," an illegal agreement in which an outside party aids in a lawsuit in order to partake in a share of the award. Connivance means to secretly allow or be involved in a wrongdoing, an immoral or illegal act.

PART TWO • Chapter 16

WORDS TO BE DEFINED

Definitions Bank	
brightly colored; radiant with light	inconspicuous; unnoticeable
to explain; to make clear	suggestive; reminding one of something
friendly; affable	various; assorted
important; well-known	

1. Jem gave Dill the histories and general attitudes of the more **prominent** figures (p. 180)
2. they pointed to Miss Maudie Atkinson's yard, **ablaze** with summer flowers (p. 181)
3. We asked Miss Maudie to **elucidate** (p. 182)
4. The Maycomb County courthouse was faintly **reminiscent** of Arlington (p. 184)
5. on the second floor, one passed **sundry** sunless county cubbyholes (p. 185)
6. I found myself in the middle of the Idlers' Club and made myself as **unobtrusive** as possible. (p. 185)
7. Judge Taylor looked like most judges I had ever seen: **amiable**, white-haired (p. 187)

 Read Chapter 16, marking the text in key places according to the method taught in "How to Mark a Book."

PART TWO • Chapter 16

COMPREHENSION QUESTIONS

1. *I was beginning to notice a subtle change in my father these days, that came out when he talked with Aunt Alexandra. It was a quiet digging in, never outright irritation.* (p. 178)

   What does Scout mean here? **Summarize** in your own words what she is saying.

2. *"First day Walter comes back to school'll be his last."* (p. 179)

   How does Atticus respond to this? Include a brief quotation in your answer.

3. What evidence in this chapter can you find for Miss Maudie's support of Atticus and his cause? Include a quotation in your answer.

4. Describe Mr. Dolphus Raymond. What makes him unique or different from the others in Maycomb? Include a brief quotation in your answer.

5. Who takes the children in to find a seat in the courthouse? Where does he take them? Is this action **symbolic**, or suggestive of something greater than just finding two open seats?

SOCRATIC DISCUSSION QUESTIONS (LOGIC | Dialectic)

1. *"Mr. Cunningham's basically a good man," he said, "he just has his blind spots along with the rest of us."* (p. 179)

   What virtue(s) does this reveal in Atticus? How is this significant to the story?

2. *"... but son, you'll understand folks a little better when you're older. A mob's always made up of people, no matter what. Mr. Cunningham was part of a mob last night, but he was still a man."* (p. 179)

   What important point is Atticus making here?

3. *"So it took an eight-year-old child to bring 'em to their senses, didn't it?" said Atticus. "That proves something — that a gang of wild animals can be stopped, simply because they're still human. Hmp, maybe we need a police force of children ... you children last night made Walter Cunningham stand in my shoes for a minute. That was enough."* (p. 179)

   What does this quote imply about children, adults, and truth?

4. *The pillars were all that remained standing when the original courthouse burned in 1856. Another courthouse was built around them. It is better to say, built in spite of them. But for the south porch, the Maycomb County courthouse was early Victorian, presenting an unoffensive vista when seen from the north. From the other side, however, Greek revival columns clashed with a big nineteenth-century clock tower housing a rusty unreliable instrument, a view indicating a people determined to preserve every physical scrap of the past.* (pp. 184-185)

   Through this description of the courthouse and its architecture, what might it be seen to **symbolize** or suggest?

5. *It was necessary to turn on the lights in the daytime; there was always a film of dust on the rough floorboards.* (p. 185)
   The Colored balcony ran along three walls of the courtroom like a second-story veranda, and from it we could see everything. (p. 187)

   Compare these two descriptions of the courtroom. Can they be read as **symbolic** or suggestive of any particular **theme** in the story?

Chapter 17

READING NOTES

1. **Mr. Horace Gilmer** – the prosecuting attorney who represents the Ewells
2. **Mr. Bob Ewell** – the father of the Ewell family; spends his welfare money on alcohol; claims to have seen Tom attacking Mayella
3. **Mayella Ewell** – the 19-year-old daughter of Bob Ewell; accuses Tom of attacking her
4. **bunged** (p. 192) – injured; damaged
5. **gullet** (p. 192) – throat
6. **bantam cock** (p. 193) – a small chicken; in this context, it means a small, but aggressive person
7. **crepey** (p. 193) – wrinkly and saggy, like crepe paper
8. **congenital** (p. 193) – inherited; hereditary
9. **gleaning** (p. 194) – collecting; gathering
10. **quelling** (p. 197) – subduing; silencing
11. **frog-sticking** (p. 201) – a method of hunting frogs with a spear or pitchfork
12. **pantomime** (p. 202) – a performance with bodily movement and gestures
13. **counting his chickens** (p. 202) – Scout uses a shortened expression of the folk saying, "Don't count your chickens before they hatch."

PART TWO • *Chapter 17*

WORDS TO BE DEFINED

Definitions Bank	
assembled; summoned	meaning; gist; sense
gently; kindly	stormy; tempestuous
harsh; bitter in language and tone	supporting; verifying
	turned; twisted

1. we saw him only when court **convened** (p. 189)
2. his chair was **skewed** to one side (p. 190)
3. With his infinite capacity for calming **turbulent** seas (p. 193)
4. he said something about **corroborating** evidence (p. 193)
5. when debate became more **acrimonious** than professional (p. 195)
6. He turned slowly in his swivel chair and looked **benignly** at the witness. (p. 195)
7. their **import** registered on his face. (p. 198)

 Read Chapter 17, marking the text in key places according to the method taught in "How to Mark a Book."

PART TWO • *Chapter 17*

COMPREHENSION QUESTIONS

1. List three details about Mr. Gilmer.
2. Who is called to the witness chair first?
3. What is Atticus's first and primary question to the sheriff?
4. List eight details about the Ewells and their living conditions. Include a quotation in your answer.
5. List two details about the African American settlement five hundred yards beyond the Ewells. Include a quotation in your answer.
6. Explain the **irony** present when you compare the Ewells and the African American settlement.
7. Describe the tone and manner of Mr. Ewell when he testifies. Include a quotation in your answer. Does he act as if he has already won the case?
8. What is Atticus's second main line of questioning? What does he uncover through this questioning?

SOCRATIC DISCUSSION QUESTIONS (LOGIC | Dialectic)

1. *Maycomb's Ewells lived behind the town garbage dump in what was once a Negro cabin.* (pp. 193-194)
   Identify the **irony** present in this particular fact about the Ewells.

2. *One corner of the yard, though, bewildered Maycomb. Against the fence, in a line, were six chipped-enamel slop jars holding brilliant red geraniums, cared for as tenderly as if they belonged to Miss Maudie Atkinson, had Miss Maudie deigned to permit a geranium on her premises.* (p. 194)
   What is the significance of these red geraniums? Can they be seen as **symbolic** in some way?

3. *All the little man on the witness stand had that made him any better than his nearest neighbors was, that if scrubbed with lye soap in very hot water, his skin was white.* (p. 195)
   Identify the **irony** in Scout's comment here.

4. *"Jedge, I've asked this county for fifteen years to clean out that nest down yonder, they're dangerous to live around 'sides devaluin' my property – "* (p. 199)
   What is **ironic** about Mr. Ewell's statement here?

5. Sheriff Tate did not call a doctor, claiming, "It wasn't necessary." How is this an example of the racism present in the community?

Chapter 18

READING NOTES

1. **lavations** (p. 203) – washings
2. **chunked** (p. 205) – a variation of the word "chucked"
3. **immaterial** (p. 208) – in court, evidence or testimony that is not essential or necessary
4. **browbeating** (p. 211) – intimidating; bullying
5. **constructionist** (p. 214) – one who interprets a law or legal document in a specified way
6. **spittoon** (p. 215) – a pot used for spitting into

WORDS TO BE DEFINED

Definitions Bank	
appeased; pacified	impartiality; the state of being neutral
elicited; called forth	
flat; emotionless	unintentional; spontaneous

1. **Mollified**, Mayella gave Atticus a final terrified glance (p. 205)
2. Judge Taylor was not the kind of figure that ever **evoked** pity (p. 207)
3. Mayella's hostility, which had subsided to grudging **neutrality**, flared again. (p. 208)
4. He did not see her **involuntary** jump, but it seemed to me that he knew she had moved. (p. 209)
5. he was speaking in his **arid**, detached professional voice. (p. 210)

 Read Chapter 18, marking the text in key places according to the method taught in "How to Mark a Book."

PART TWO • Chapter 18

COMPREHENSION QUESTIONS

1. How old is Mayella?
2. Why do you think Mayella takes such offense at Atticus calling her "ma'am" or "Miss Mayella"?
3. Is there any evidence in Mayella's responses to Atticus that her father has beaten her? Include a brief quotation of Mayella in your answer.
4. What aspects of Mayella's answers about her being beaten around the face suggest that she is not telling the truth? Include a brief quotation of Mayella in your answer.
5. What physical drawback makes it highly unlikely that Tom could physically beat and rape Mayella? Include a brief quotation in your answer.
6. When Atticus rains several questions on Mayella about her attacker, how does she respond? What is it about her reaction that suggests Atticus's questions "hit her hard"? (p. 214)
7. When Mayella finally speaks after Atticus's numerous questions, what does she say to the jury that would not be acceptable in the court of law today? Include a quotation in your answer.

SOCRATIC DISCUSSION QUESTIONS (LOGIC | Dialectic)

1. *Apparently Mayella's recital had given her confidence, but it was not her father's brash kind: there was something stealthy about hers, like a steady-eyed cat with a twitchy tail.* (p. 206)

   Relate this quote to the central **symbol** of the mockingbird. Is there anything suggestive about Lee's use of this particular **simile** here?

2. How do you feel about Mayella? Does she also deserve sympathy? Why or why not?

Chapter 19

READING NOTES

1. **Mr. Link Deas** – Tom and Helen Robinson's employer; stands up for their character by shouting out from the audience in court
2. **testimony** (p. 218) – a formal spoken or written statement
3. **ex cathedra** (p. 222) – with authority that comes from one's position or office

WORDS TO BE DEFINED

Definitions Bank	
choice; decision	to eliminate completely; to erase
difficult situation; mess	
disrespectful; offensively bold	not diminished or weakened
	persuaded; convinced

1. Atticus very quickly **induced** him to tell us (p. 216)
2. He … would never go up into somebody's yard of his own **volition**. (p. 219)
3. I did not understand the subtlety of Tom's **predicament** (p. 221)
4. His speech was miraculously **unimpaired** by his cigar. (p. 222)
5. Judge Taylor told the reporter to **expunge** anything he happened to have written down (p. 222)
6. Are you being **impudent** to me, boy? (p. 225)

Read Chapter 19, marking the text in key places according to the method taught in "How to Mark a Book."

PART TWO • Chapter 19

COMPREHENSION QUESTIONS

1. List two biographical details about Tom Robinson.
2. Describe the character of Tom Robinson. What kind of person is he? List three examples that reveal his character. Include a brief quotation in your answer.
3. What bold action does Mr. Link Deas take in the courtroom? Include a brief quotation in your answer. What happens as a result?
4. Describe the attitude and tone of Mr. Gilmer. What words, phrases, and statements in his questioning of Tom reveal his culturally entrenched racism? Include a few quotations in your answer.
5. What is Dill's reaction to Mr. Gilmer's cross-examination? What does this reveal about Dill?
6. What important point does Scout realize about Atticus as a lawyer and person in talking with Dill outside the courthouse? Provide a direct quotation for your answer.

SOCRATIC DISCUSSION QUESTIONS (LOGIC | Dialectic)

1. *As Tom Robinson gave his testimony, it came to me that Mayella Ewell must have been the loneliest person in the world.* (p. 218)

    Why does Scout say this? Include a quotation in your answer. Do you agree with her?

2. *Tom Robinson was probably the only person who was ever decent to her. But she said he took advantage of her, and when she stood up she looked at him as if he were dirt beneath her feet.* (p. 218)

    Summarize what Scout is saying. What are the crucial issues here?

3. *It occurred to me that in their own way, Tom Robinson's manners were as good as Atticus's. Until my father explained it to me later, I did not understand the subtlety of Tom's predicament ...* (p. 221)

    What is Tom's predicament? How is he caught between two impossible options?

Chapter 20

READING NOTES

1. **corroborative evidence** (p. 230) – additional evidence that supports a proof already offered
2. **dictated** (p. 230) – said or read aloud
3. **minute sifting of complicated facts** (p. 231) – a close scrutiny of numerous complicated facts
4. **all men are created equal** (p. 233) – a key phrase from The Declaration of Independence
5. **asyndeton** – a rhetorical device in which one or several conjunctions are omitted in order to create energy or emphasis
6. **adianoeta** – a kind of irony; an expression that, in addition to the obvious meaning, carries a second, subtle meaning (often at variance with the ostensible meaning)[1]

WORDS TO BE DEFINED

Definitions Bank	
an extremely small amount	not softened or lessened; unrelieved
formerly charged with a serious crime	committed; carried out (esp. a deception or crime)
illegal or prohibited goods	
reckless boldness	

1. I had never encountered a being who deliberately **perpetrated** fraud against himself. (p. 228)
2. this man was **indicted** on a capital charge and is now on trial for his life (p. 230)
3. The state has not produced one **iota** of medical evidence (p. 231)
4. But in this case she was no child hiding stolen **contraband** (p. 231)
5. who had the **unmitigated** temerity to "feel sorry" for a white woman (p. 232)
6. who had the unmitigated **temerity** to "feel sorry" for a white woman (p. 232)

---

[1]. "Adianoeta." Silva Rhetoricae. http://rhetoric.byu.edu/Figures/A/adianoeta.htm

PART TWO • Chapter 20

 Read Chapter 20, marking the text in key places according to the method taught in "How to Mark a Book."

COMPREHENSION QUESTIONS

1. What surprise do the children discover about Mr. Dolphus Raymond? Why does he do this?

2. *"Cry about the simple hell people give other people — without even thinking. Cry about the hell white people give colored folks, without even stopping to think that they're people, too."* (p. 229)

    What important point is Mr. Dolphus making here? **Summarize** what he is saying.

3. *"This case is as simple as black and white."* (p. 231)

    How is Atticus's statement **ironic** and an example of **adianoeta**?

4. *"The state has not produced one iota of medical evidence to the effect that the crime Tom Robinson is charged with ever took place."* (p. 231)

    What evidence has the state relied on instead? You may quote Atticus in your answer.

5. *"I say guilt, gentlemen, because it was guilt that motivated her. She has committed no crime, she has merely broken a rigid and time-honored code of our society, a code so severe that whoever breaks it is hounded from our midst as unfit to live with."* (p. 231)

    When Mayella broke the rigid, time-honored code of showing romantic interest in a person of a different race, what does Atticus say she did to deal with the problem?

6. What did Mr. Bob Ewell most likely do when he saw his daughter make a romantic pass at Tom? What evidence does Atticus present that strongly supports this?

7. What important point does Atticus make about the general human race and particular races?

8. Where does Atticus say is the one place in this country that all men are created equal?

SOCRATIC DISCUSSION QUESTIONS (LOGIC | Dialectic)

1. *I had a feeling that I shouldn't be here listening to this sinful man who had mixed children and didn't care who knew it, but he was fascinating. I had never encountered a being who deliberately perpetrated fraud against himself. But why had he entrusted us with his deepest secret?* (p. 228)
   What, in Scout's words, gives the indication that she is growing in awareness and understanding?

2. How does Mr. Dolphus answer the children when they ask him why he shared his deepest secret with them? Include a quotation. What important point is conveyed in his answer?

3. *"Thomas Jefferson once said that all men are created equal .... There is a tendency in this year of grace, 1935, for certain people to use this phrase out of context, to satisfy all conditions. The most ridiculous example I can think of is that the people who run public education promote the stupid and idle along with the industrious — because all men are created equal, educators will gravely tell you, the children left behind suffer terrible feelings of inferiority. We know all men are not created equal in the sense some people would have us believe — some people are smarter than others, some people have more opportunity because they're born with it, some men make more money than others, some ladies make better cakes than others — some people are born gifted beyond the normal scope of most men."* (p. 233)
   Summarize Atticus's words here. What general point is he making? Do you agree? Why or why not?

4. How does Atticus define the *court* by way of logical reasoning? Explain what he means.

Chapter 21

READING NOTES

1. **peeved** (p. 236) – annoyed; irritated
2. **droves** (p. 236) – a large group of people moving or acting as a body
3. **paralysis** (p. 236) – the inability to act or function
4. **psychical research** (p. 239) – the investigation of events that appear to be contrary to physical laws and suggest the possibility of mental activity that exists apart from the body

WORDS TO BE DEFINED

Definitions Bank	
angry; offended	objected; took issue with
easing up; slackening	revenge; retaliation
to find one not guilty; to exonerate	

1. we could tell Atticus was **relenting**. (p. 236)
2. You think they'll **acquit** him that fast? (p. 236)
3. The streetlights were on, and we glimpsed Calpurnia's **indignant** profile (p. 236)
4. Calpurnia served Jem, Dill and me with a **vengeance**. (p. 237)
5. "Mr. Jem," Reverend Sykes **demurred**, "this ain't a polite thing for little ladies to hear …" (p. 238)

PART TWO • Chapter 21

 Read Chapter 21, marking the text in key places according to the method taught in "How to Mark a Book."

COMPREHENSION QUESTIONS

1. What does Atticus tell the children to do when he discovers they've been up in the balcony all afternoon? What does he agree to let them do?
2. Describe the courtroom when the children return from dinner. You may include a quotation in your answer.
3. At about what time did Mr. Tate announce that the court should come to order?
4. After the verdict is announced, what action displays the great respect the African American community has for Atticus?

PART TWO • *Chapter 21*

SOCRATIC DISCUSSION QUESTIONS (LOGIC | Dialectic)

1. *I was exhilarated. So many things had happened so fast I felt it would take years to sort them out, and now here was Calpurnia giving her precious Jem down the country — what new marvels would the evening bring?* (pp. 236-237)

    Describe the feelings and thoughts of Scout. Does she seem like she is growing in understanding and maturity?

2. Why do you think Calpurnia does not want the children to be at the trial?

3. *The old courthouse clock suffered its preliminary strain and struck the hour, eight deafening bongs that shook our bones.* (p. 239)

    How is the clock **symbolic** of the courtroom situation? How is **onomatopoeia** used to convey the feelings of those present in the courtroom?

4. *He said if enough people — a stadium full, maybe — were to concentrate on one thing, such as setting a tree afire in the woods, that the tree would ignite of its own accord. I toyed with the idea of asking everyone below to concentrate on setting Tom Robinson free, but thought if they were as tired as I, it wouldn't work.* (p. 239)

    How is this passage a kind of illustration of Harper Lee's hope? Do you think she is saying something to America in her time?

5. *But I must have been reasonably awake, or I would not have received the impression that was creeping into me. It was not unlike one I had last winter, and I shivered, though the night was hot. The feeling grew until the atmosphere in the courtroom was exactly the same as a cold February morning, when the mockingbirds were still, and the carpenters had stopped hammering on Miss Maudie's new house, and every wood door in the neighborhood was shut as tight as the doors of the Radley Place.* (pp. 239-240)

    How does the use of **similes** and **symbolism** help convey the mood in the courtroom?

6. *What happened after that had a dreamlike quality ...* (p. 240)

    When the jury returns, why does Scout say that the subsequent events have a dreamlike quality? Can you relate to Scout's feeling? Have you experienced a situation like this?

Chapter 22

READING NOTES

1. **glistened** (p. 242) – shined; sparkled
2. **missionary teas** (p. 243) – the ladies Missionary Society charity events
3. **cynical** (p. 244) – distrustful of human sincerity or integrity
4. **feral** (p. 245) – fierce; vicious
5. **bridgework** (p. 245) – dentures

WORDS TO BE DEFINED

Definitions Bank	
despondent because of a belief that all things are inevitable and cannot be changed	gloomily; somberly
	lifted; hauled
expressing sorrow or regret	showing little emotion; expressionless

1. his collar and tie were neatly in place, his watch-chain glistened, he was his **impassive** self again. (p. 242)
2. "Atticus—" said Jem **bleakly**. (p. 243)
3. Jem groaned and **heaved** himself up from the swing. (p. 245)
4. "Don't you oh well me, sir," Miss Maudie replied, recognizing Jem's **fatalistic** noises (p. 246)
5. Jem grinned **ruefully**. (p. 246)

 Read Chapter 22, marking the text in key places according to the method taught in "How to Mark a Book."

PART TWO • *Chapter 22*

COMPREHENSION QUESTIONS

1. *Our father sighed. "I'm going to bed," he said. "If I don't wake up in the morning, don't call me." (p. 243)*
   Atticus deserves a long night of sleep. Does he get one?
2. What surprises Atticus in the morning when he sees Calpurnia in the kitchen? Describe some of the items. How does Atticus respond?
3. According to Dill, what is Miss Rachel's reaction to the verdict?
4. In his dialogue with Aunt Alexandra, what evidence do we find that Dill has grown in wisdom and understanding? Include a quotation in your answer.
5. What gossipy comments and questions does Miss Stephanie say were all over town the next morning?
6. Who in the community of Maycomb does Miss Maudie identify as having a true Christian perspective like Atticus?
7. What did Judge Taylor do to help the cause of justice in the Tom Robinson case?
8. Provide a quotation of Miss Maudie that conveys her optimism about the verdict.
9. What does Bob Ewell do when he sees Atticus the day after the trial?

PART TWO • *Chapter 22*

SOCRATIC DISCUSSION QUESTIONS (LOGIC | Dialectic)

1. *"This is their home, sister," said Atticus. "We've made it this way for them, they might as well learn to cope with it."*
   "But they don't have to go to the courthouse and wallow in it —"
   "It's just as much Maycomb County as missionary teas." (p. 243)

   Aunt Alexandra chastises Atticus by saying that the children should be sheltered from the hypocrisy of the Maycomb courthouse. Atticus responds that the hypocrisy is not only in the Maycomb courthouse, but in the high-society ladies Missionary Society. Aunt Alexandra is a "missionary teas" sort of lady.

   Do you think the children should be exposed to the ugly hypocrisy of the Maycomb trial, or kept sheltered? Why or why not?

2. *"How could they do it, how could they?"*
   "I don't know, but they did it. They've done it before and they did it tonight and they'll do it again and when they do it — seems that only children weep. Good night." (p. 243)

   Summarize this quote. What does this suggest about children and their purity of heart?

3. What great compliment does Miss Maudie say about Atticus in her discussion with the children? Provide a quotation of her comment. Do you agree with her? Why or why not?

4. *"Well I'm gonna be a new kind of clown. I'm gonna stand in the middle of the ring and laugh at the folks."* (p. 247)

   Identify the **symbolic** implications of Dill's interest in becoming a clown. What important point does he make through this **imagery**?

Chapter 23

READING NOTES

1. **Old Sarum** – An area in northern Maycomb County, where the Cunninghams are from. When Boo Radley was younger, he ran into some trouble with a rowdy group from Old Sarum.
2. *Popular Mechanics* (p. 250) – a classic magazine of popular technology, first published in 1902
3. **"He'll go to the chair"** (p. 250) – the electric chair; used for capital execution by electricity
4. **circumstantial evidence** (p. 251) – Indirect evidence that relies on a series of facts other than the particular fact sought to be proved. The series of facts, by reason and experience, is so closely connected to the fact to be proved (e.g., the person committed the crime) that the fact may be strongly inferred from the existence of the circumstantial evidence.
5. **stolidly** (p. 252) – showing little or no emotion
6. **square deal** (p. 252) – fair deal
7. **leastways** (p. 257) – at least
8. **hipped** (p. 258) – very absorbed or interested
9. **epiphany** – a moment of insight, discovery, or revelation

PART TWO • Chapter 23

WORDS TO BE DEFINED

Definitions Bank	
childish; immature	secretive; done by stealth
determined; forceful	seedy; debased
distinctly; with clear perception	strategies; plans
removed; pulled out	

1. "Something **furtive**," Aunt Alexandra said. "You may count on that." (p. 250)
2. I guess it's to protect our frail ladies from **sordid** cases like Tom's. (p. 252)
3. Our **stout** Maycomb citizens aren't interested, in the first place. (p. 253)
4. I was reminded **vividly** of the last time she had put her foot down. (p. 255)
5. This time the **tactics** were different, but Aunt Alexandra's aim was the same. (p. 256)
6. "Have a chew, Scout." Jem dug into his pocket and **extracted** a Tootsie Roll. (p. 256)
7. Jem waved my question away as being **infantile**. (p. 258)

 Read Chapter 23, marking the text in key places according to the method taught in "How to Mark a Book."

PART TWO • *Chapter 23*

COMPREHENSION QUESTIONS

1. How did Atticus respond to the verbal abuse from Bob Ewell?
2. When Jem expresses his concern about Bob Ewell to Atticus, what advice does Atticus give to Jem?
3. What hope does Atticus provide for his children regarding Tom Robinson? Include a quotation in your answer.
4. What is Atticus's primary misgiving about the death penalty?
5. *"You couldn't, but they could and did. The older you grow the more of it you'll see."* (p. 252)

   What does Atticus say Jem will see more of as he grows older?
6. What other issue of discrimination does Lee take up regarding the composition of juries in Alabama at this time?
7. How does Aunt Alexandra feel about Scout getting together with Walter Cunningham? For your answer, provide a quotation by Aunt Alexandra that encapsulates her perspective.

PART TWO • Chapter 23

SOCRATIC DISCUSSION QUESTIONS (LOGIC | Dialectic)

1. *"But lots of folks have been hung – hanged – on circumstantial evidence," said Jem.*
   "I know, and lots of 'em probably deserved it, too – but in the absence of eyewitnesses there's always a doubt, sometimes only the shadow of a doubt. The law says 'reasonable doubt,' but I think a defendant's entitled to the shadow of a doubt. There's always the possibility, no matter how improbable, that he's innocent." (p. 251)

   Do you agree with Atticus concerning his disapproval of the death penalty based on purely circumstantial evidence? Why or why not?

2. *"Those are twelve reasonable men in everyday life, Tom's jury, but you saw something come between them and reason."* (p. 251)

   Explain what Atticus means in this paragraph. What is it that comes between the men and reason?

3. *"You've many more miles to go, son."* (p. 253)

   What does Atticus mean through this **metaphor**? What is Atticus's main point here about serving on juries? Include a quotation. Do you agree with Atticus?

4. *"I didn't say not to be nice to him. You should be friendly and polite to him, you should be gracious to everybody, dear. But you don't have to invite him home."* (p. 256)

   Assess this statement by Aunt Alexandra. Do you have any problems with what she says? Or do you agree with her? Explain.

5. *"There's four kinds of folks in the world."* (p. 258)
   "Naw, Jem, I think there's just one kind of folks. Folks." (p. 259)

   Jem divides Maycomb county into four kinds of people. Scout argues for one kind. But does Jem actually agree with Scout? Whose perspective does Harper Lee advocate? Whom do you think is correct?

6. What does Jem mean by relating his **epiphany** that Boo Radley wants to stay inside?

Chapter 24

READING NOTES

1. **Mrs. Grace Merriweather** – a "devout" Methodist and member of Aunt Alexandra's missionary circle
2. **Gertrude Farrow** – another lady at the missionary circle; "the second most devout lady in Maycomb"
3. **squalid** (p. 260) – dirty; wretched; despicable
4. **Mrunas** – an African tribe
5. **Barker's Eddy** – a local creek and swimming hole
6. **nome** (p. 262) – a contraction for "no, m'am"
7. **sibilant** (p. 265) – characterized by a hissing, *s* or *sh* sound
8. **bovine** (p. 265) – cowlike; of, or relating to, cattle

WORDS TO BE DEFINED

Definitions Bank	
anxiety; fear	rudeness; disrespect
began; started	something said in a slow, dignified style
compulsion; coercion	
not delightful or pleasant	suspended; postponed

1. Immediately thereafter, the ladies **adjourned** for refreshments. (p. 261)
2. Ladies in bunches always filled me with vague **apprehension** and a firm desire to be elsewhere (p. 262)
3. you've already **commenced** going to court. (p. 262)
4. Miss Stephanie eyed me suspiciously, decided that I meant no **impertinence** (p. 263)
5. Mr. Merriweather, a faithful Methodist under **duress** (p. 263)
6. "Nothing, Jean Louise," she said, in stately **largo** (p. 264)
7. no matter how **undelectable** they were, there was something about them that I instinctively liked (p. 267)

PART TWO • *Chapter 24*

 Read Chapter 24, marking the text in key places according to the method taught in "How to Mark a Book."

COMPREHENSION QUESTIONS

1. List three details about Mrs. Grace Merriweather.
2. What does Scout say about "ladies in bunches"? Why does she feel this way?
3. In whose world does Scout say she feels more at home? Why do you think she feels this way? Include a quotation in your answer.
4. What did Tom lose the day they took him to prison?
5. *He stopped in the doorway. His hat was in his hand, and his face was white.* (p. 268)

    What grave news does Atticus bring?
6. Provide the quotation by Atticus that offers a forthright explanation as to why Tom chose to escape.
7. According to Miss Maudie, what does she, Atticus, and a few others — "the handful of people" — believe? Include a quotation in your answer.

PART TWO • Chapter 24

SOCRATIC DISCUSSION QUESTIONS (LOGIC | Dialectic)

1. *Today Aunt Alexandra and her missionary circle were fighting the good fight all over the house.* (p. 260)
   Identify the **sarcasm** in Scout's description.

2. *"Jean Louise," she said, "you are a fortunate girl. You live in a Christian home with Christian folks in a Christian town. Out there in J. Grimes Everett's land there is nothing but sin and squalor."* (p. 264)
   Identify the **irony** in Mrs. Merriweather's comment.

3. Find two more examples of **irony** from Mrs. Merriweather's comments and quote them below.

4. Identify an example of **adianoeta** (an ironic kind of double statement) in the words of Scout when she describes Mrs. Merriweather.

5. *Mrs. Merriweather nodded wisely. Her voice soared over the clink of coffee cups and the soft bovine sounds of the ladies munching their dainties.* (p. 265)
   How does Lee present another irony in the diction above?

6. How are the names of Mrs. Farrow and Mrs. Merriweather examples of an **ironic pun** or **adianoeta**?

PART TWO • *Chapters 12-24*

Rhetoric | Expression

*Express in your own words the Central
One Idea with supporting points.*

RHETORICAL EXPRESSION:
To be answered in your Literature Notebook in preparation for your essay.

1. In 2-3 paragraphs, **summarize** the major events of Part Two (Chapters 12-24).

2. Write the **Central One Idea** of Part Two in a precise, eloquent sentence.

3. List three or four points that support your determination of the Central One Idea.

4. Write a **lead** (1-2 sentences) that grabs the reader's attention—such as a *quote, question, startling fact or statistic, scenario, piece of dialogue,* etc.

5. Write an **amplification/importance** (1-2 sentences) that explains why your thesis is important in a larger or more universal sense.

◆ **Central Quote:** *Choose a quote from anywhere in Part Two that you think best embodies the Central One Idea and copy it down.*

❶ **Write the Central One Idea as expressed by the teacher.**

ESSAY OPTION

Choose a topic below and respond with a 3-5 paragraph essay that includes an Introduction with a clear thesis; a Body with organized, logical, and specific support of the thesis; and a Conclusion with an amplification of the thesis/support.

The essay should feature appropriate tone, voice, and point of view; correct grammar, usage, and mechanics; a variety of sentence structures enhanced by subordination and parallelism; a balance of general and specific detail; and enhanced rhetorical effect through transition words, appropriate diction, strong verbs, descriptive adjectives, and other rhetorical devices.

Note: Some of these prompts tend toward a shorter essay, and some toward a longer. Check with your teacher to see what length he or she suggests. Both short essays (1 page) and long essays (2-4 pages) are useful and helpful, depending on the intent and purpose.

1. Discuss the effects of racism on the citizens of the town of Maycomb. You may look closely at a couple citizens, such as Tom Robinson and Mayella Ewell, or you may look at a larger number of citizens, such as Tom, Atticus, Calpurnia, Dolphus Raymond, Scout, Jem, Dill, Bob Ewell, etc. — or any combination thereof.

2. Write an essay about Tom Robinson and his various qualities. Take a clear position on his character, defending it with evidence from the text, as well as your own logical conclusions and perceptions.

3. Now that you have read through Chapter 24, you have seen Atticus in fuller detail. Write an essay about Atticus and his various qualities. Take a position about Atticus as a father, leader, or person (or all three), and support your thesis with evidence from the text. Note: If you wrote about Atticus for Part One, you may write about him again, but it should be a new essay with new evidence and ideas.

4. Write an essay about Scout's movement from childhood innocence to the wisdom and understanding of adulthood. Discuss her gradual enlightenment, supported by key moments from the text up to this point. If you wrote about Scout in Part One, you should write a new essay here and extend or expand upon your ideas from Part One.

PART TWO • Chapters 12-24

5. What does the novel have to say about courage? How is courage defined in the text? What characters embody true courage?

6. Select a quote by Atticus that you think is the wisest and most important. Place that quote at the top of your page and write an essay on why the quote is true, and why it is important.

7. *As Tom Robinson gave his testimony, it came to me that Mayella Ewell must have been the loneliest person in the world. She was even lonelier than Boo Radley, who had not been out of the house in twenty-five years.* (p. 218)

    Write an essay about Mayella Ewell. What kind of person is she? What has her life been like? How much is she to blame for falsely accusing Tom? How much does her background figure in to her decision?

8. [Central One Idea] Use the Central One Idea of Part Two as your thesis, and support it with some evidence from your reading of Part Two and/or your work in the Literature Notebook.

9. [Open] Write an essay in which you analyze an aspect of Part Two that is of import to you, such as a particular theme, character, setting, element of plot, dialogue, symbol, or other literary or rhetorical motif.

10. [Teacher] Essay prompt.

PART THREE
Chapters 25-31

PRE-GRAMMAR | Preparation
Prepare to think about the novel and its Central One Idea by drawing upon my prior knowledge, experience, or interests.

1. Write about a time when you made a set of assumptions or judgments about someone. Why did you make those assumptions? Were you able to get to know the person, or become aware of his or her background? Did your assumptions change after you got to know him or her? What did you learn in this process?

GRAMMAR | Presentation
LOGIC | Dialectic

In the Grammar section, discover essential facts, elements, and features of the novel through the Reading Notes, Words to Be Defined, and Comprehension Questions.

In the Logic section, reason with the facts, elements, and features of the novel; sort, arrange, compare, and connect ideas — and begin to uncover and determine the Central One Idea.

Chapter 25

READING NOTES

1. **roly-poly** (p. 272) – a small insect that can roll into a ball
2. **scampered** (p. 274) – ran away with quick, light steps
3. **editorial** (p. 275) – a newspaper article written by the editor that gives an opinion on an issue

WORDS TO BE DEFINED

Definitions Bank	
death; passing; termination	high probability that something will occur; likelihood
nauseated; sickening	
	promises; pledges

1. He had left us the first of the month with firm **assurances** that he would return (p. 273)
2. the **prospect** of walking all the way back home at dusk, when the traffic is light, is tiresome (p. 273)
3. The name Ewell gave me a **queasy** feeling. (p. 276)
4. Maycomb had lost no time in getting Mr. Ewell's views on Tom's **demise** (p. 276)

 Read Chapter 25, marking the text in key places according to the method taught in "How to Mark a Book."

PART THREE • *Chapter 25*

COMPREHENSION QUESTIONS

1. Briefly describe how Atticus told Mrs. Robinson about Tom's death. What happened in that scene?
2. How does Mr. Underwood feel about Tom's death? Include a quotation in your answer.
3. Identify two **metaphors** that Scout uses in the final paragraph of this chapter.

SOCRATIC DISCUSSION QUESTIONS (LOGIC | Dialectic)

1. Can the roly-poly be understood in a way that is similar to the mockingbird? Why or why not? Explain.
2. According to Scout, what does Mr. Underwood say in his editorial that reiterates the **motif** of the mockingbird? Include a quotation.
3. *Then Mr. Underwood's meaning became clear: Atticus had used every tool available to free men to save Tom Robinson, but in the secret courts of men's hearts Atticus had no case. Tom was a dead man the minute Mayella Ewell opened her mouth and screamed.* (pp. 275-276)

   Summarize what Scout means, giving particular attention to "the secret courts of men's hearts." Does Scout have a kind of **epiphany** here? If so, what is her new insight?

Chapter 26

READING NOTES

1. **Miss Gates** – Scout's third grade teacher
2. **Adolf Hitler** – the Nazi dictator of Germany from 1933-1945
3. **democracy** (p. 281) – government by the people, exercised directly or through elected representatives
4. **dictatorship** (p. 281) – government by one person, a dictator, who has absolute power
5. **lest** (p. 283) – for fear that

WORDS TO BE DEFINED

Definitions Bank	
not genuine or authentic	pronounced clearly and distinctly
one who lives a solitary life and avoids others; a hermit	supposedly; reportedly
physical or mental pain	

1. I sometimes felt a **twinge** of remorse (p. 277)
2. what reasonable **recluse** wants children peeping through his shutters (p. 277)
3. This practice **allegedly** overcame a variety of evils (p. 279)
4. a publication **spurious** in the eyes of Miss Gates, our teacher (p. 279)
5. "... Pre-ju-dice," she **enunciated** carefully. (p. 281)

 Read Chapter 26, marking the text in key places according to the method taught in "How to Mark a Book."

COMPREHENSION QUESTIONS

1. What grades are Jem and Scout in at the start of this school year?
2. Is Scout's perspective of Boo changing a little? What evidence can you find that might suggest this?
3. What does Scout discover about Atticus that surprises her? Include a quotation in your answer.

SOCRATIC DISCUSSION QUESTIONS (LOGIC | Dialectic)

1. Do the citizens of Maycomb, despite appearances, actually respect Atticus? Why or why not?
2. What is the chief **irony** in the chapter? Explain in detail. Include a quotation in your answer.
3. Does Scout discover or question the **irony** that you discussed in the previous question? How so? Include a quotation in your answer.
4. *"But it's okay to hate Hitler?"*
   "It is not," he said. "It's not okay to hate anybody." (p. 282)

   Do you agree with Atticus? Or do you think it is okay to hate somebody like Hitler? Why or why not?

PART THREE • *Chapter 27*

Chapter 27

READING NOTES

1. **Misses Tutti and Frutti Barber** – maiden ladies, sisters, who live together in Maycomb; hard of hearing, if not deaf, and have a cellar in their house
2. **annals** (p. 284) – historical records
3. **Works Progress Administration (WPA)** (p. 284) – a large federal employment act initiated in the 1930s that employed millions of unemployed people to carry out public-works projects
4. **carcass** (p. 286) – a body, living or dead
5. **Ladies' Law** (p. 286) – a law in Alabama introduced in 1907 that made it illegal to use any abusive, obscene, or threatening language within earshot of a girl, woman, or someone's house
6. **Cotton Tom Heflin** (p. 287) – J. Thomas "Cotton John" Heflin was a Democratic congressman and senator from Alabama. He was a leading proponent of white supremacy, and drew many of his votes from the Ku Klux Klan.
7. **National Recovery Act** (p. 288) – a series of programs enacted to help the nation's businesses recover from the Great Depression
8. **dog Victrolas** (p. 288) – the advertising logo of RCA/Victor records, featuring a dog looking into a large Victrola (gramaphone)
9. *Ad Astra Per Aspera* (p. 289) – a Latin phrase meaning "Through difficulties to the stars"

WORDS TO BE DEFINED

> **Definitions Bank**
>
> ornate; elaborate
> secretively; furtively
> speaking in a soft, low voice
> surrounded by; in the middle of
> the state of being well known for bad qualities or misdeeds
> thieved; stole

1. his job only lasted as long as his **notoriety** (p. 284)
2. and received it with no grace **amid** obscure mutterings (p. 284)
3. One Sunday night, lost in fruity metaphors and **florid** diction (p. 285)
4. she heard a soft voice behind her, **crooning** foul words. (p. 286)
5. wicked children … **stealthily** made away with every stick of furniture (p. 288)
6. Miss Tutti was sure those traveling fur sellers who came through town two days ago had **purloined** their furniture. (p. 289)

 Read Chapter 27, marking the text in key places according to the method taught in "How to Mark a Book."

PART THREE • *Chapter 27*

COMPREHENSION QUESTIONS

1. What was the second unusual thing that happened in Maycomb in October?
2. What was the third unusual thing that happened? How was it resolved?
3. What explanation does Atticus give to Scout to help explain Bob Ewell's aggressive behavior toward those connected with the case? Include a quotation in your answer.
4. What did some Maycomb kids do for a prank on Halloween the previous year?
5. What are Mrs. Grace Merriweather's plans for the children in the pageant?

SOCRATIC DISCUSSION QUESTIONS (LOGIC | Dialectic)

1. What two incidents or comments toward the end of this chapter **foreshadow** that something bad might happen? You may include a direct quotation in either of your descriptions.

Chapter 28

READING NOTES

1. **Cecil Jacobs** – a schoolmate of Scout and Jem's; scares them on the way to the Halloween pageant
2. **haint** (p. 292) – a Southern colloquialism for ghost
3. **repertoire** (p. 293) – the full range of songs that a singer can sing (or scenes that an actor can perform, etc.)
4. **gait** (p. 293) – manner of walking
5. **homemade divinity** (p. 295) – a soft, creamy candy
6. **climbers** (p. 295) – people trying to move up the social ladder
7. **lichen** (p. 296) – a combination of green algae and fungal tissue that grows on trees

WORDS TO BE DEFINED

Definitions Bank	
ancient; primitive	high-pitched; piercing
completely free; unrestricted	humiliation; shame; wounded pride
filled with; swarming	
gentlemanly; chivalrous	quick-tempered; irritable

1. I thought it **gallant** of him to do so. (p. 292)
2. plunging from the **shrill** kee, kee of the sunflower bird (p. 293)
3. kee of the sunflower bird to the **irascible** qua-ack of a bluejay (p. 293)
4. the hall was **teeming** with slicked-up country people. (p. 294)
5. entangled his troops so far northwest in the forest **primeval** (p. 296)
6. I could hide my **mortification** under it. (p. 297)
7. He liked to tell things his own way, **untrammeled** by state or defense (p. 305)

PART THREE • *Chapter 28*

 Read Chapter 28, marking the text in key places according to the method taught in "How to Mark a Book."

COMPREHENSION QUESTIONS

1. Describe the **setting** in this chapter. Include a quotation. What makes the setting ominous?
2. Who surprises Scout and Jem on their way to the auditorium?
3. Describe two activities that the children do in the auditorium before the pageant.
4. Scout describes many details and features of the pageant. Choose a couple sentences of description that stand out to you and quote them below.
5. Describe Mrs. Merriweather's and Jem's reactions to Scout's performance on stage (her late entrance).
6. Provide three quotes that serve as good examples of the **rising action** that leads to the **climax** of Part Three, Bob Ewell's attack.
7. What does Scout think about "the man who brought Jem in … standing in a corner, leaning against the wall"? Include a quotation.
8. List all of the adults in the room when Scout and Jem are being treated for injuries.
9. What do we learn about Bob Ewell from Mr. Heck Tate at the end of the chapter?

PART THREE • Chapter 28

SOCRATIC DISCUSSION QUESTIONS (LOGIC | Dialectic)

1. *We laughed. Haints, Hot Steams, incantations, secret signs, had vanished with our years as mist with sunrise.* (p. 292)
   Write the **simile** in the quote above. How does the **simile** help convey that Scout and Jem are growing up?

2. *High above us in the darkness a solitary mocker poured out his repertoire in blissful unawareness of whose tree he sat in ...* (p. 293)
   What is the "solitary mocker"? Provide a brief **summary** of the quote above. Does this **imagery** carry any **symbolic** significance?

3. Consider the events of Scout and Jem's trip to the pageant, such as the **setting** of darkness, the root that trips Scout, and Cecil Jacobs scaring them. Do these function as elements of **foreshadowing**? Explain.

Chapter 29

READING NOTES

1. **mantelpiece** (p. 306) – a structure of wood, marble, metal, or stone above or around a fireplace
2. **hidy** (p. 309) – a variant of *howdy*, which means "hello"

WORDS TO BE DEFINED

Definitions Bank	
in an overly showy, gaudy manner	to rebuke; to scold
pierced with little holes	shy; apprehensive

1. His sleeves were **perforated** with little holes. (p. 308)
2. but brought my arm down quickly lest Atticus **reprimand** me for pointing. (p. 310)
3. so white they stood out **garishly** against the dull cream wall in the dim light (p. 310)
4. His lips parted into a **timid** smile, and our neighbor's image blurred with my sudden tears. (p. 310)

 Read Chapter 29, marking the text in key places according to the method taught in "How to Mark a Book."

PART THREE • *Chapter 29*

COMPREHENSION QUESTIONS

1. Why does Mr. Tate want them to stay in the bedroom, rather than move to the livingroom as Aunt Alexandra suggests?
2. What thing in particular does Mr. Tate say saved Scout's life?
3. How did Scout know she was under the tree when she "couldn't see thunder out there." For your answer, provide a quotation of Scout's response.
4. *"Why there he is, Mr. Tate, he can tell you his name."* (p. 309)

   To whom is Scout referring? List three details from the text that describe him.

SOCRATIC DISCUSSION QUESTIONS (LOGIC | Dialectic)

1. *"Mr. Finch, there's just some kind of men you have to shoot before you can say hidy to 'em. Even then, they ain't worth the bullet it takes to shoot 'em. Ewell 'as one of 'em."* (pp. 308-309)

   Summarize the context of this quote. Why does Mr. Heck Tate say this?

2. *… but as I gazed at him in wonder the tension slowly drained from his face. His lips parted into a timid smile, and our neighbor's image blurred with my sudden tears.* (p. 310)

   Why is Scout struck with emotion when she discovers that the man is Boo Radley? How would you feel in that moment?

Chapter 30

READING NOTES

1. **astounded** (p. 311) – amazed; astonished
2. **scat** (p. 312) – Go away!; Leave me alone.
3. **competent** (p. 315) – adequate; reasonable
4. **craw** (p. 316) – the stomach of any animal

WORDS TO BE DEFINED

Definitions Bank	
determinedly; firmly fixed	smoothly; pleasantly in manner
remained; awaited	separated; released from something that entangles
secretly allowed; conspired	

1. If Atticus could **blandly** introduce me to Boo Radley at a time like this, well—that was Atticus. (p. 311)
2. Mr. Heck Tate sat looking **intently** at Boo through his horn-rimmed glasses. (p. 311)
3. if I **connived** at something like this, frankly I couldn't meet his eye (p. 314)
4. Honed it down and **bided** his time ... just bided his time. (p. 316)
5. Atticus **disengaged** himself and looked at me. (p. 317)

 Read Chapter 30, marking the text in key places according to the method taught in "How to Mark a Book."

PART THREE • Chapter 30

COMPREHENSION QUESTIONS

1. Why does Scout lead Boo to the chair on the deck farthest from Atticus and Mr. Tate?
2. Whom does Atticus initially think caused Bob Ewell's death? And when he thinks this, what does he insist upon that further attests to his character?
3. Include a short quotation by Atticus that you think best encapsulates his character in his discussion with Mr. Heck Tate.
4. Who is Mr. Heck Tate really trying to protect? Why? Include a quotation in your answer.

SOCRATIC DISCUSSION QUESTIONS (LOGIC | Dialectic)

1. *Well, it'd be sort of like shootin' a mockingbird, wouldn't it?* (p. 317) The mockingbird **motif** recurs again here. How would reporting Boo's involvement be "sort of like shooting a mockingbird"? In other words, why does Scout say this?

Chapter 31

READING NOTES

1. **raling** (p. 318) – a harsh, crackling respiratory sound arising in a cough
2. **body English** (p. 319) – body language
3. **auxesis** – A rhetorical device in which words or clauses are arranged in increasing intensity of meaning and force. It is a kind of *climax, incrementum,* or *amplification.*
4. **polysyndeton** – The use of several conjunctions in close succession. Example: "He ran *and* jumped *and* laughed for joy."

WORDS TO BE DEFINED

Definitions Bank	
outlined or shaped against a different colored background	perceptive; intelligent
	stopped abruptly; ceased
anxious; fearful	

1. I led him to the front porch, where his uneasy steps **halted**. (p. 319)
2. They stopped at an oak tree, delighted, puzzled, **apprehensive**. (p. 321)
3. his children shivered at the front gate, **silhouetted** against a blazing house (p. 321)
4. He was **shrewd(er)** than I, however: the moment I sat down I began to feel sleepy. (p. 321)

 Read Chapter 31, marking the text in key places according to the method taught in "How to Mark a Book."

PART THREE • Chapter 31

COMPREHENSION QUESTIONS

1. Scout is finally able to fulfill her childhood wish to meet Boo Radley. How is he different than what she had long-assumed?

2. *"Will you take me home?"* (p. 319)

   What does Boo sound like when he asks Scout to take her home? Provide a quotation and underline or highlight the **metaphor**.

3. Why does Scout insist that she not lead Boo home, but he lead her to his home?

4. Describe some of Scout's memories as she returns home. Why is she so nostalgic at this time?

5. *"Besides, nothin's real scary except in books."* (p. 322)

   Why do you think Scout says this?

6. Identify the use of **polysyndeton** in the scene when Atticus begins to read to Scout. Quote it below. How does this contribute to the **mood** or feeling of the scene?

PART THREE • Chapter 31

SOCRATIC DISCUSSION QUESTIONS (LOGIC | Dialectic)

1. *Neighbors bring food with death and flowers with sickness and little things in between.* (p. 320)
   Summarize Scout's reflection about neighbors and neighborly giving. You may include a quotation in your summary. What important realization, or **epiphany**, does Scout have when thinking about this? How does she feel about this realization?

2. Identify the **auxesis** in the paragraph about neighbors and quote it below.

3. *I turned to go home. Street lights winked down the street all the way to town. I had never seen our neighborhood from this angle. There was Miss Maudie's, Miss Stephanie's — there was our house, I could see the porch swing — Miss Rachel's house was beyond us, plainly visible. I could even see Mrs. Dubose's.* (p. 320)
   This passage contains a great number of references to seeing and perspective. What do you think Harper Lee's intent was here? How might this relate to the Central One Idea of the novel?

4. *Atticus was right. One time he said you never really know a man until you stand in his shoes and walk around in them. Just standing on the Radley porch was enough.* (p. 321)
   Why does Scout recall and affirm what Atticus said at this moment from the Radley porch? How does it relate to the **Central One Idea** of the novel?

5. *The street lights were fuzzy from the fine rain that was falling. As I made my way home, I felt very old ...* (p. 321)
   Why does Scout feel old on her walk home? How does this relate to the **Central One Idea**?

6. In the closing scene, when Atticus walks Scout to bed in her sleepy state, does Scout mumble her way to the **Central One Idea** of the novel? Does Atticus's response help convey this? Explain.

PART THREE • Chapters 25-31

Rhetoric | Expression

*Express in your own words the Central
One Idea with supporting points.*

RHETORICAL EXPRESSION:

To be answered in your Literature Notebook in preparation for your essay.

1. In 2-3 paragraphs, **summarize** the major events of Part Three (Chapters 25-31).

2. Write the **Central One Idea** of the novel in a precise, eloquent sentence.

3. List three or four points that support your determination of the Central One Idea for the novel.

4. Write a **lead** (1-2 sentences) that grabs the reader's attention—such as a *quote, question, startling fact or statistic, scenario, piece of dialogue,* etc.

5. Write an **amplification/importance** (1-2 sentences) that explains why your thesis is important in a larger or more universal sense.

◆ **Central Quote:** *Choose a quote from anywhere in Part Three that you think best embodies the Central One Idea and copy it down.*

❶ **Write the Central One Idea as expressed by the teacher.**

PART THREE • Chapters 25-31

ESSAY OPTION

Choose a topic below and respond with a 3-5 paragraph essay that includes an Introduction with a clear thesis; a Body with organized, logical, and specific support of the thesis; and a Conclusion with an amplification of the thesis/support.

The essay should feature appropriate tone, voice, and point of view; correct grammar, usage, and mechanics; a variety of sentence structures enhanced by subordination and parallelism; a balance of general and specific detail; and enhanced rhetorical effect through transition words, appropriate diction, strong verbs, descriptive adjectives, and other rhetorical devices.

Note: Some of these prompts tend toward a shorter essay, and some toward a longer. Check with your teacher to see what length he or she suggests. Both short essays (1 page) and long essays (2-4 pages) are useful and helpful, depending on the intent and purpose.

1. Research the Civil Rights movement of the 1950s and 1960s. Write an informative essay about the movement. Your essay should have an introduction with a clear thesis, 3-5 body paragraphs, each explaining an important aspect of the Civil Rights movement, and a conclusion.

2. *People moved slowly then. They ambled across the square, shuffled in and out of the stores around it, took their time about everything. A day was twenty-four hours long but seemed longer. There was no hurry, for there was nowhere to go, nothing to buy and no money to buy it with, nothing to see outside the boundaries of Maycomb County.* (p. 6)

   The novel is set in the 1930s during the Great Depression. Research the Great Depression and write an informative essay about the Great Depression and its effect on the country during that time. Your essay should have an introduction with a clear thesis, 3-5 body paragraphs, each explaining an important aspect of the Great Depression, and a conclusion.

3. The novel presents some important concepts about the ideals of womanhood. Write an essay in which you state and analyze what you think the novel asserts or questions about womanhood. You will want to consider important characters, conversations, and moments in the story to build and support your argument.

4. Write an essay on the role that Calpurnia, or Miss Maudie, or both, play in the life of Scout.

5. Choose one of the essay prompts (that you did not already write about) from the essay section at the end of Part Two.

6. [Central One Idea] Use the Central One Idea of the novel as your thesis, and support it with some evidence from your reading of the novel and/or your work in the Literature Notebook.

7. [Open] Write an essay in which you analyze an aspect of the novel that is of import to you, such as a particular theme, character, setting, element of plot, dialogue, symbol, or other literary or rhetorical motif.

8. [Teacher] Essay prompt.

Memorization & Recitation

INSTRUCTIONS:

Select a passage (or 2-3 small passages from different places) from *To Kill a Mockingbird* that you particularly like or feel some connection to. Follow the steps below to memorize the passage(s). In your Literature Notebook, practice writing the passage(s) to help you memorize it, as the steps below explain. After you have memorized the entire passage, write your *final handwritten version* in your best penmanship on a new page in your Literature Notebook.

You have 3 choices regarding the number of lines and the letter grade:

A: 17-20 lines   B: 12-16 lines   C: 9-11 lines

HOW TO MEMORIZE A PASSAGE

1. **Read the passage several times in order to understand the passage and its main idea.**
   - It is much easier to memorize something you understand!
   - Read the passage both silently and aloud.
2. **Get to know the rhythm, tone, and general structure of the passage.**
   - Knowing the rhythm and sound of the passage will increase your ability to remember it.
3. a. **Read the first sentence several times until you memorize it.** (both silently and aloud)
   b. **Read the second sentence a number of times until you memorize it.** (both silently and aloud)
   c. **Recite the two sentences together.** (both silently and aloud)
   d. **Repeat steps a-c for the next two sentences.**
   e. **Write the four sentences down with good penmanship.**
4. **Repeat steps a-e for each set of four sentences.**
5. **After memorizing each set of four sentences, recite the previous four sentences and the new four sentences together.** (both silently and aloud)
6. **Continue until the entire passage is memorized.**
7. **Have your parent, sibling, or friend sit down and listen to you recite your passage!**
8. **Be sure to ask your teacher to set aside a class session for everyone to recite his or her passage!**

Master Words-to-Be-Defined List

PART 1

1. abominable
2. accosted
3. ambled
4. analogous
5. antagonized
6. apoplectic
7. apprehensively
8. articulate
9. ascertaining
10. asinine
11. auspicious
12. bade
13. beckoning
14. benevolence
15. burdensome
16. commotion
17. condescended
18. condescension
19. conferred
20. cordial
21. degeneration
22. desolate
23. diminutive
24. disapprobation
25. dispensation
26. edification
27. erratic
28. erratically
29. evasion
30. expounding
31. foliage
32. guilelessness
33. impotent
34. imprudent
35. inconspicuous
36. indigenous
37. ingenuous
38. iniquities
39. innate
40. inordinately
41. inquisitive
42. invective
43. magisterial
44. malevolent
45. malignant
46. meddling
47. meditative
48. melancholy
49. murmur
50. nebulous
51. nocturnal
52. obliged
53. perpetual
54. perplexity
55. placidly
56. predilection
57. provocation
58. quelling
59. ramshackle
60. reconnaissance
61. scurrying
62. sojourn
63. tacit
64. tarnished
65. tirade
66. tranquil
67. umbrage
68. vapid
69. vehemently
70. vexations
71. wallowing
72. waning
73. wrought

PART 2

1. ablaze
2. acquit
3. acrimonious
4. adjourned
5. affliction
6. amiable
7. apprehension
8. arid
9. austere
10. begrudge
11. benignly
12. bleakly
13. commenced
14. contraband
15. convened
16. corroborating
17. customary
18. demurred
19. denoted
20. denunciation
21. dignity
22. duress
23. elucidate
24. elusive
25. encumbered
26. evoked
27. expunge
28. extracted
29. fatalistic
30. formidable
31. fortitude
32. frivolous
33. furtive
34. heaved
35. impassive
36. impertinence
37. import
38. impudent
39. inaudible
40. indicted
41. indignant
42. induced
43. infallible
44. infantile
45. invoke
46. involuntary
47. iota
48. largo
49. mollified
50. myopic
51. neutrality
52. obliquely
53. perpetrated
54. predicament
55. prerogative
56. prominent
57. relenting
58. reminiscent
59. resilient
60. ruefully
61. skewed
62. sordid
63. stifle
64. stout
65. succinct
66. sundry
67. tactful
68. tactics
69. temerity
70. tentative
71. turbulent
72. undelectable
73. unimpaired
74. unmitigated
75. unobtrusive
76. venerable
77. vengeance
78. vividly
79. volition

PART 3

1. allegedly
2. amid
3. apprehensive
4. assurances
5. bided
6. blandly
7. connived
8. crooning
9. demise
10. disengaged
11. enunciated
12. florid
13. gallant
14. garishly
15. halted
16. intently
17. irascible
18. mortification
19. notoriety
20. perforated
21. primeval
22. prospect
23. purloined
24. queasy
25. recluse
26. reprimand
27. shrewd(er)
28. shrill
29. silhouetted
30. spurious
31. stealthily
32. teeming
33. timid
34. twinge
35. untrammeled

Rhetoric Essay Template

I. **INTRODUCTION**

  A. **Lead:** Grab the reader's attention with a *quote, question, startling fact or statistic, scenario, piece of dialogue,* etc.

  B. **Short Summary:** In a paragraph, **summarize** the section or work.

  C. **Central One Idea:** Write the Central One Idea (your thesis) in a complete sentence.

II. **SUPPORT (BODY PARAGRAPHS):** List 3 points of support, using bullet points. Each of these bullet points will become a body paragraph.

  A.

  B.

  C.

III. **AMPLIFICATION / IMPORTANCE:** Write the last sentence or two of your conclusion, explaining why your thesis is important in a larger or more universal sense.